NIGHTLY WISDOM

NIGHTLYWISDOM

BUDDHIST INSPIRATIONS FOR SLEEPING, DREAMING, AND WAKING UP

edited by Josh Bartok

compiled by Gustavo Szpilman Cutz

WISDOM PUBLICATIONS • BOSTON

Wisdom Publications
199 Elm Street, Somerville MA 02144 USA • www.wisdompubs.org

Library of Congress
Cataloging-in-Publication Data
Nightly wisdom : Buddhist inspirations for sleeping, dreaming, and waking up / edited by Josh Bartok ; compiled by Gustavo Szpilman Cutz.
 p. cm.
 Includes bibliographical references and index.
 ISBN 0-86171-549-7 (pbk. : alk. paper)
 1. Spiritual life—Buddhism. 2. Sleep—Religious aspects—Buddhism. 3. Dreams—Religious aspects—Buddhism. 4. Wakefulness. I. Bartok, Josh. II. Cutz, Gustavo Szpilman.
 BQ5675.N55 2007
 294.3'442—dc22
                                    2007036419
ISBN 0-86171-549-7

12 11 10 09 08
5   4   3   2   1

2LR-2OT.2OM

Cover design by
Interior design by Gopa & Ted2, Inc.
Set in Weiss 11/15.

Wisdom Publications' books are printed on acid-free paper and meet the guidelines for permanence and durability of the Production Guidelines for Book Longevity of the Council on Library Resources.

Printed in the United States of America

This book was produced with environmental mindfulness. We have elected to print this title on 50% PCW recycled paper. As a result, we have saved the following resources: 34 trees, 23 million BTUs of energy, 2,960 lbs. of greenhouse gases, 12,287 gallons of water, and 1,578 lbs. of solid waste. For more information, please visit our website, www.wisdompubs.org.

TABLE OF CONTENTS

PREFACE

Human beings the world over have always found the nighttime—
and its attendant activities of sleeping, dreaming, and waking
up—mysterious and rich with mystical possibility. The Buddhist
tradition has explored this realm in particular detail. In fact, the
name Buddha means simply "the one who has awakened" and
enlightenment itself is often literarily portrayed as the radiant full
moon, lighting our way through the blinding black of night.
Buddhist masters have for centuries held out the intriguing
possibility that sleep itself can be yet another form of practice,
another field for us to cultivate wisdom and compassion, while
playing freely in the samadhi of dream.

Nightly Wisdom goes deep into the wealth of Buddhist
inspirations on these powerful topics, offering encouragement
and clear teaching on lucid dreaming and Tibetan "dream yoga";
gentle guidance on relaxing into restful sleep and awakening from
the suffering dream of separateness; as well as nighttime poetry
and prose whose sources span time and space from ancient Asia
and the Buddha himself to some of the brightest lights in
Buddhism's Western skies.

I invite you to place *Nightly Wisdom* on your bedside table, so that you can make a practice of reading a passage or two before you close your eyes for the evening. Let the sage words of these accomplished explorers of the mind sink in, and let your sleep be suffused with a virtue that can be renewed in the morning and carried on throughout each day.

May this book become a helpful guide, a trusted companion, for anyone who has ever dreamed of waking up to the entirety of life or wondered how to best fill with luminous wisdom that third of our lives we all spend in bed.

Josh Bartok
Wisdom Publications
Somerville, Massachusetts

We all sleep.
Whether we acknowledge it or not we all dream.
And certainly every single one of us will die.
Although these issues affect us all, they retain a sense
of mystery and fascination.

Mara the Evil One, on finding the Blessed One lying down mindfully after enduring, without becoming distressed, severe pains from a cut made on his foot by a stone splinter, said:
> "Do you lie down in a daze or drunk on poetry?
> Don't you have sufficient goals to meet?
> Alone in a secluded lodging
> Why do you sleep with a drowsy face?"

The Blessed One:
> "I do not lie in a daze or drunk on poetry;
> Having reached the goal, I am rid of sorrow.
> Alone in a secluded lodging
> I lie down full of compassion for all beings.
>
> "Even those with a dart stuck in the breast
> Piercing their heart moment by moment—
> Even these here, stricken, get to sleep;
> So why should I not get to sleep
> When my dart has been drawn out?

"I do not lie awake in dread,
Nor am I afraid to sleep.
The nights and days do not afflict me,
I see for myself no decline in the world.
Therefore I can sleep in peace,
Full of compassion for all beings."

Then Mara the Evil One, realizing, "The Blessed One knows me, the Fortunate One knows me," sad and disappointed, disappeared right there.

All subjects and objects in the dream can be transformed. In dream yoga you may take a hundred things and transform them into just one, or take one thing and multiply it by a hundred. This is the practice that Milarepa did during the waking state, when he emanated innumerable forms of a certain object. In one particular account, he emanated himself inside a yak horn, without the yak horn getting bigger or him getting smaller. That is an indication that he was extremely well versed in dream yoga.

As the familiar daytime aspects of things are gradually lost in the great fragrant darkness, the question of faith grows more distinct, more urgent, for we begin to perceive around us what cannot be relied on or revered as unchangeable and secure; namely, all of this that we can point to, label, and define, all conditioned, compounded things, however beautiful or alive with the evening's mystery.

When I was a student, my first meditation teacher gave me some practical advice. He began by asking me the first thing I did after getting up in the morning.

"I go to the bathroom," I said.

"Is there a mirror in your bathroom?" he enquired.

"Of course."

"Good," he said. "Now, every morning, even before you brush your teeth, I want you to look in that mirror and smile at yourself."

"Sir!" I began to protest. "I am a student. Sometimes I go to bed very late, and get up in the morning not feeling my best. Some mornings, I would be frightened to look at myself in a mirror, let alone smile!"

He chuckled, looked me in the eye, and said, "If you cannot manage a natural smile, then take your two index fingers, place one on each corner of your mouth, and push up. Like this." And he showed me.

He looked ridiculous. I giggled. He ordered me to try it. So I did.

The very next morning, I dragged myself out of bed and staggered to the bathroom. I looked at myself in the mirror. "Urrgh!" It was not a pretty sight. A natural smile was a nonstarter. So I took my two index fingers, placed one on each corner of my mouth, and pushed up. I then saw this stupid young guy making a silly face in the mirror, and I couldn't help grinning. Once there was a natural smile, I saw the student in the mirror smiling at me. So I smile even more. The man in the mirror smiled even more. In a few seconds, we ended up laughing together.

I continued that practice every morning for two years. Every morning, no matter how I felt when I got out of bed, I was soon laughing at myself in the mirror, usually with the help of my two fingers. People say I smile a lot these days. Perhaps the muscles around my mouth got kind of stuck in that position.

Experiences in a dream are not true, because after waking from sleep not even a trace of them having happened is apparent. They are also not false, because they were experienced during the dream.

Sleep, wake, sleep, wake, until the sleeper wakes no more. Without attention, without the particular turnings of attention developed and practiced through meditative consciousness, forgotten dreams and too-soon forgotten days seem likely all there is: unawakened mind.

The energy necessary to awaken constantly leaks away from us, morning till night. As we struggle to hold our lives together—trying to win, trying to please, trying to hide, trying to avoid discomfort—our energy is dissipated in mindless chatter, needless action, wanton daydreams. We rage, we lust, we fear. We gossip, complain, dramatize; we fidget, tense, strain; we fantasize and worry. Above all we try to plan for the unknowable. And all the while the very energy that could fuel our awakening leaks away, drop by drop. Our task is to learn to stop these leaks.

EZRA BAYDA WITH JOSH BARTOK IN *SAYING YES TO LIFE*

By examining diverse appearances, the meditator will experience the indivisible union of appearance and its intrinsic emptiness as being devoid of any identifiable essence. This union of mind and appearance should be understood to be like the union between the consciousness in a dream and its appearance. For instance, in a dream the emergence of diverse appearances is not different from the mind's unceasing manifestation. The emergence of the diverse appearances and the mind should, therefore, be understood as being an indivisible union.

There is said to be a relationship between dreaming, on the one hand, and the gross and subtle levels of the body on the other. But it's also said there is such a thing as a "special dream state." In that state, the "special dream body" is created from the mind and from vital energy within the body. This special dream body is able to disassociate entirely from the gross physical body and travel elsewhere.

Those who can remain in meditation while in dreamless sleep have the potential to abide in the realization of the nature of the clear light of sleep. For an ordinary person, the many dreams that occur during the course of the night are produced by latent predispositions, or mental imprints. These come from the activation of the three poisons of greed, anger, and ignorance, which, in turn, stem from a lack of realization of the two types of identitylessness (of persons and of phenomena).

On one occasion the Blessed One was dwelling at
Rajagaha in the Bamboo Grove, the Squirrel Sanctuary.
Then, when the night was fading, the Blessed One,
having spent much of the night walking back and forth in
the open, washed his feet, entered his dwelling, and lay
down on his right side in the lion's posture, with one leg
overlapping the other, mindful and clearly
comprehending, having attended to the idea of rising.

Then Mara the Evil One approached the Blessed One
and addressed him in verse:

"What, you sleep? Why do you sleep?
What's this, you sleep like a wretch?
Thinking 'The hut's empty' you sleep:
What's this, you sleep when the sun has risen?"

The Blessed One:

"Within him craving no longer lurks,
Entangling and binding, to lead him anywhere;

With the destruction of all acquisitions
The Awakened One sleeps:
Why should this concern you, Mara?"

Then Mara the Evil One, realizing, "The Blessed One knows
me, the Fortunate One knows me," sad and disappointed,
disappeared right there.

Not a single one of any of the dreams I had last night remains when I wake up. Likewise, not a single one of all these daytime appearances today will appear tonight in my dreams. There is no difference between the dreams of the day and the night.

PADMASAMBHAVA QUOTED IN *THE ATTENTION REVOLUTION*

The most profound and effective way to overcome sloth and torpor is to stop fighting your mind. Stop trying to change things and instead let things be. Make peace, not war, with sloth and torpor. Then your mental energy will be freed to flow into the knower, and your sloth and torpor will naturally disappear.

A state called *witnessing deep sleep* is described as dreamless sleep in which you experience a quiet, peaceful inner state of awareness or wakefulness—a feeling of infinite expansion and bliss, and nothing else. Then, one becomes aware of one's own existence as an individual—which may lead to emerging from sleep.

Although everyone can dream, not all dreams are significant; and some dreams—those that suggest the presence of other realms—need to be understood and incorporated into waking reality.

Overnight in Ch'eng-Hsiang Forest

We're visiting together
when the sun goes down,
in a forest of a thousand trees
not yet bare of leaves.

A rock-tangled creek
flows out the valley;
mountain rain
drips on a perching owl.

Around our lamp,
we hear the water clock flow;
thanks to the host,
the guest stays up late.

We enjoyed
this evening fully;
but…ah,
if the moon had shone.

When we have a nightmare, such as dreaming we are being burned by a big fire, we can wake up in fright. Even though that fire does not truly exist as it seems to in the dream, it will produce fear as the result. In the same way, the tortures of the hot and cold hells experienced by the hell-denizens as a result of their previous actions do not inherently exist, yet the experience of pain, suffering, and terror resulting from these tortures does exist.

GESHE LHUNDUB SOPA, MICHAEL SWEET, AND LEONARD ZWILLING
IN *PEACOCK IN THE POISON GROVE*

If we fall asleep with a virtuous or noble frame of mind, then the odds are higher that the first thought that springs to mind when we wake up will also be virtuous or noble. That is one aspect of karma—the karmic result of consciously planting a thought in our mind. As a result of that first conscious thought, a new thought may occur that is a reflection of that first thought. It's not the same thought, but something that feels quite similar due to the power of what preceded it. That is how habits are formed. If you fall asleep feeling deeply unhappy, then the moment you wake up there will be some remnant of that feeling. It's not likely if you go to sleep feeling sad that you will wake up feeling full of joy. Isn't that true?

Dreaming can be viewed as the special case of perception without the constraints of external sensory input. Conversely, perception can be viewed as the special case of dreaming constrained by sensory input.

Let's say it's a dark night, and in this total darkness we are dreaming, or experiencing a dream world. The mental space where the dream takes place—independent of the physical place where we are—could be compared to the openness of mind, while its capacity for experiencing, despite the external darkness, corresponds to its clarity. This lucidity encompasses all mind's knowledge and is the clarity inherent in these experiences. It is also the lucidity of what or who experiences them; knower and known, lucidity and luminosity are but two facets of the same quality. As the intelligence that experiences the dream, it is lucidity, and as the clarity present in its experiences, it is luminosity. But at the nondual level of pure mind, it is one and the same quality: "clarity." This example may be helpful in understanding, but bear in mind that it is just an illustration showing at a habitual level a particular manifestation of clarity. In the example, there is a difference between the lucidity of the knower and the luminosity of that subject's experiences. This is because the dream is a dualistic experience, differentiated in terms of subject and object, in which clarity manifests itself at once in the awareness or lucidity of the subject and in the luminosity of its objects.

From *Song of the Twelve Hours of the Day*

Middle of the night—the first hour
In my dreams, I go here and there and don't know how
　　to stop myself.
Treading into pieces the green of the eastern hills and
　　the western peaks,
Then turning over to find one's been nestled in the
　　bedcovers all along.

The cock crows—the second hour
All the routines of everyday life, each one naturally in
　　accord.
Over there, by the banks of the river, they scrub their
　　faces until they shine,
Over here, rinsing the mouth with tea then swallowing
　　it down....

The sun rises—the fourth hour
In the coral tree groves, the colors are bright
    and radiant.
There is no need to look elsewhere for the Buddha,
    Gautama,
His sixteen-foot-tall golden body is in a single blade of
    grass.

When the World-Honored One was in the world,
the asura king Rahula wanted to swallow the moon.
The heavenly moon was frightened and appeared before
Buddha and recited to Buddha this verse, "World-
Honored Buddha of great wisdom and pure effort,
now I take refuge and make prostrations. This Rahula
is upsetting me. I entreat the Buddha to look upon me
with pity, and help and protect me."

The Buddha recited a verse to the asura king Rahula
saying, "The moon can illuminate the darkness, pure and
cool. This is the great bright lamp in the empty sky.
Its color is white and pure with a thousand rays. Do not
swallow the moon, but immediately release it." At this
time the asura king Rahula sweated with fear and shame,
immediately letting go of the moon.

The night receives in silence the cricket's call and our own speechless questions.

Why do we sleep and dream? What is the purpose of it?
There is quite a debate in neuroscience about this, but
there are fundamentally two ways of answering the
question. Some people think of sleep as a form of
restoration or replenishment. But while this feels
intuitively true, nobody so far has identified precisely
what it is that we are replenishing. You spend a lot of
energy during sleep; there is actually more oxygen
consumed during REM sleep than when awake, so it's not
a simple matter of letting the machine cool off. Because
REM is such an active state, it's not obvious how we are
replenishing, restoring, or refreshing ourselves.

The other answer, which I personally prefer, is that
REM sleep is a fundamental cognitive activity. It is the
place where people can engage in imaginary play, trying
out different scenarios, learning new possibilities; a space
of innovation where new patterns and associations can
arise, where whatever was experienced can be elaborated.
Dreaming provides a space where you don't just cope

with immediacy, but instead can reimagine, reconceive, reconceptualize. It allows you to come up with new possibilities.

A friend awoke one morning from one of those dreams that was so vivid it seemed real. He had dreamt that five angels had given him five big jars of gold worth a fortune. When he opened his eyes, there were no angels in his bedroom and, alas, no pots of gold. But it was a very strange dream.

When he went into the kitchen, he saw that his wife had made him five boiled eggs with five pieces of toast for his breakfast. At the top of the morning newspaper he noticed the date, the fifth of May (the fifth month). Something odd was surely going on. He turned to the back pages of the newspaper, to the horseracing pages. He was stunned to see that at a racetrack called Ascot (five letters), in race number five, horse number five was called…Five Angels! The dream was clearly an omen.

He took the afternoon off work. He drew five thousand dollars out of his bank account. He went to the race-track, to the fifth bookmaker and made his bet: five thousand dollars on horse number five, race number five, Five Angels, to win.

The dream couldn't be wrong. The lucky number five couldn't be wrong! And indeed the dream wasn't wrong. The horse came in fifth.

When you go to bed in the evening, cultivate the Spirit of Awakening, thinking, "For the sake of all sentient beings throughout space, I shall practice the illusion-like samadhi, and I shall achieve perfect buddhahood. For that purpose, I shall train in dreaming." Then as you lie down, rest on your right shoulder, with your head pointing north, your right hand pressed against your cheek, and your left placed upon your thigh. Clearly imagine your body as your chosen deity.

Rest without clinging.

A *lucid dream* is a dream in which one is actively aware of the fact that one is dreaming. In such a dream, one can even begin to manipulate the story and the characters to create a desired situation. For example, in an unpleasant dream situation, the dreamer might reflect, "I don't have to put up with this," and then change the dream or at least back out of the involvement. *Witnessing dreaming* is a dream in which you experience a quiet, peaceful inner awareness or wakefulness, completely separate from the dream.

JAYNE GACKENBACH IN *SLEEPING, DREAMING, AND DYING*

Strive diligently, with no distinction of day and night.

Gampopa was having a lot of very strange and vivid dreams. When he asked Milarepa about them, Milarepa replied, "You are a great teacher of the Kadampa and you must have heard and studied the Buddha's teachings extensively. Do you not remember that the Buddha said that dreams are merely illusions, that in fact dreams exemplify the state of illusion? Was the Buddha joking when he said this?" Milarepa went on to explain, "When we meditate, many new experiences arise in our mind, because we are working with our mind in a new way. There is no reason to be elated by pleasant experiences or depressed by unpleasant ones."

To apprehend the clear light in the nature of reality itself, you who nakedly identify awareness should position your body as before, subdue your awareness, and in vivid clarity and emptiness focus your awareness at your heart, and fall asleep. When your sleep is agitated, do not lose the sense of indivisible clarity and emptiness. When you are fast asleep, if the vivid, indivisibly clear and empty light of deep sleep is recognized, the clear light is apprehended. One who remains without losing the experience of meditation all the time while asleep, without the advent of dreams or latent predispositions, is one who dwells in the nature of the clear light of sleep.

How can one increase lucidity in one's dreams?
One can do things before going to sleep, such as
cultivating the intention for lucidity. Meditation is
another possibility; some people will wake up about
three-quarters of the way through their sleep cycle, at
about four o'clock in the morning, meditate, and go back
to sleep. That seems to help.

In desiring to wake up, resolve to arise in time the next morning and to practice. Go to sleep for a moderate time in order to enhance your physical well-being, since a proper rest nurtures the generative elements in the body. While sleeping, visualize a disc of light on which to focus. This will prevent darkness from descending on the mind, render the sleep light, allow you to wake up in time, energetic for the morning meditation.

Further along in my psychoanalytic training, while I was still working on the koan Mu, I had an unusual dream: Walking along a familiar street, I suddenly came upon my own dead body in the gutter. Astonished, I bent down to see if that's what it really was. As I did so, a black-robed figure appeared and asked me my name. "Barry Magid," I answered. Pointing to the corpse, the figure again asked my name, and again I answered, "Barry Magid." A third time, the figure pointed to the dead body and again asked my name. This time I could only reply, "I don't know." Then the figure said, "You can have anything you want." I was dumbstruck and didn't know what to ask for, when I noticed he was now holding a can of soda. I pointed to that and asked for a sip, which he gave me. I then walked away, dazzled by the sunlight on the street.

Even taken out of its original context, I think we can see how this dream might portend the sudden dissolution of an old sense of who I was, the "death" of an old identity, and the emergence of a new, more open sense of self and possibility. But what brought it about? And what relationship did the dream's message have to the interpretations I was used to hearing from my analyst? In the case of this particular dream, I remember, my analyst offered no interpretation at all—except for a big smile.

A Dream Journey to Mount Tiantai

Across the Stone Bridge I soared until I came
    to the Lotus Throne,
Wandering through halls and towers, I saw
    firsthand the supreme causes.
When a fragrant vapor suffused my clothes,
    for the first time I felt cleansed,
When the sound of a bell reached my ears, in
    a split second, I was dust-free.
The wooden lad and the stone maiden, the
    host within the guest,
Green bamboo and yellow blossoms, I now
    see what they mean.
Recalling the past, I lean into the wind and let
    out three long sighs;
On the azure waters, the bright moon's
    reflection glows like a jewel.

In contrast to lucid dreaming, *witnessing dreaming* is an experience of quiet, peaceful inner awareness or wakefulness, completely separate from the dream. In witnessing dreaming it's said that the person *can* manipulate the dream, but simply has no wish to do so. Whatever the content of the dream is, one feels an inner tranquillity of awareness that's removed from the dream. Sometimes one may even get caught up in the dream, but the inner awareness of peace remains.

Before leaving home, the Buddha had the following dreams, which are the dreams all buddhas have just before they leave home:

1. He saw his hands and feet stir the water of the four great oceans, and the whole earth became a well-adorned bed with Mount Meru as a pillow.

2. He saw a light spread throughout the world, dispelling darkness, and a parasol came out of the earth, spreading light in the three worlds and extinguishing suffering.

3. Four black and white animals licked his feet.

4. Birds of four colors became a single color.

5. He climbed a mountain of repulsive dung, and was not soiled by it.

Spending the Night at a Villager's Pavilion

The pillow for his bed
is a rock from mid-stream;

the spring from the well-bottom
flows to a pond through bamboo.

The night is half gone,
but the guest hasn't slept;

he alone hears
the mountain rain arrive.

Everyone who has had a dream can understand how, during that state, we are conscious of the appearance of many things that seem to be very real. This is so much the case that we react to them with all kinds of emotions, treating them as though they were external and as though our own existence were somehow dependent on interaction with them. We dream of a tiger coming after us and respond with fear and a desire to escape, but when we awake, we realize that the tiger never had a speck of true reality, being nothing more than a projection of mind. Our responses to such appearances are altogether erroneous; the mind simply doesn't recognize their true reality as, for example, mere dream tigers projected by the mind itself.

At this time when the transitional process of dreaming
   is appearing to me,
I shall abandon negligence and the cemetery of delusion.
With unwavering mindfulness, I shall enter the experience
   of the nature of being.
Apprehending the dream-state, I shall train in emanation,
   transformation, and the clear light.
I will not sleep like an animal,
But practice integrating sleep and direct perception!

Just before falling asleep there's always a final thought. We can try to make that last thought a noble, benevolent thought. If we can do that, the quality of that thought can permeate our entire sleeping state. The possibility is there. We can then say, from a spiritual point of view, that our sleep has become a virtuous sleep.

Likewise, you could just doze off without any particular frame of mind—not evil, not noble, just neutral. If that happens the sleeping state will not have any particular benefit or harm. If your last thought is selfish, or even hostile, then falling asleep with that in mind saturates the sleeping state with unwholesome emotions. This is a simple idea, but it is an important one. Without too much difficulty, without too much hardship, we can ensure that a significant portion of our lives becomes saturated with goodness. Isn't that a pleasant idea?

When we wake up in the morning, where are all the people we were just dreaming about? Where did they come from? And where did they go? Are they real or not? Of course not. These dream people and their dream experiences all arose from our sleeping, dreaming mind; they were mere appearances to that mind. They were real only as long as we remained in the dream-state; to the waking mind of the next morning they are only an insubstantial memory. While we were asleep they seemed so true, as if they were really out there, having concrete existence quite apart from ourselves. But when we wake up we realize that they were only the projections of our dreaming mind. Despite how real they seemed, these people in fact lack even an atom of self-existence. Completely empty of any objective existence whatsoever, they were only the hallucination of our dream experience.

In a very similar way, everything we experience while we are awake, including our strong sense of self, is also empty of true existence.

Which Is Real?

Your signless love circles my youth like a faintly swaying
     gauze curtain
   that wraps itself around a young girl's dream.
Pulsating—young bloods dance to heaven's clear music.
Panting—little should sleep in the shade of heaven's
   falling flowers.

Endless threads of attachment bind my sleep,
   as spring rain turns to blue haze amid the drooping
   willows.
A short dream struggles under the quilt, trying to follow
   the wind.
Desperate dream-cries stifle my throat, calling to people
   across the river.
Shattered moonbeams splinter dew-wet flowers like
   broken rice,

and the bitterness of your parting turns into a sharp knife
that cuts me to the bone.
The stream outside the gate doesn't need my tears
to swell its flow.
The mad wind in the spring hills waits for my sighs and
gathers strength to shake the flowers.

In a further stage of dream yoga you release the dream, letting it vanish back into the space of the mind, and rest in a silent, luminous awareness of awareness itself, devoid of any other content. This is the state of lucid dreamless sleep, and in this state you may apprehend the substrate consciousness, and possibly even pristine awareness.

For this, the daytime practice of *shamatha without a sign* (in which the attention is not directed to anything, but rests in its own nature) is an excellent preparation.

That night when we met
to make love in my dreams, I willed
to be a never-awakened one,
though it's said that
everlasting night's a miserable fate.

Shakyamuni Buddha saw the morning star and was enlightened, and he said, "I and the great earth and beings simultaneously achieve the Way."

Who is the first person you are aware of when you wake up in the morning? You! Do you ever say, "Good morning, me. Have a nice day!"? I do. Who is the last person you are aware of when you go to sleep? Yourself again! I say goodnight to myself. I give myself importance in the many private moments of my day. It works.

We have received a gift of Dhamma from the Buddha, passed down through all these centuries of sorrow, and it illuminates what once was dark and fearful. This mortal body moves on through the pleasant evening—and this is a happy opportunity to observe—but mind goes farther, or can go farther, into astounding distances of insight, sailing on faith and knowledge toward a brighter country.

You must come to know mind and perception
as indistinguishable, like the mind of the dreamer
and the dream's appearances.

Perhaps the function of waking is to elaborate who and how I may be in my dreams. The lucid dreamer is not dreaming to live life while awake, but, with preternatural agency and choice, is living life while asleep.

We can't wake up simply by wishing to. Without specific, ongoing effort we will continue to sleepwalk through our self-centered dream. Genuine awakening requires bringing attention repeatedly to the present moment of our life. One laserlike tool to help us do this is the practice of continually asking ourselves, "What is this?" Used in this way, the question becomes a koan, and as with all koans, the "answer" can never be conceptual. Don't try to analyze what the moment is about. Instead, fully feel the texture of what your life truly is right now. The only real answer to the question "What is this?" is your immediate experience itself.

One method used to instruct a person in practicing dream yoga is to instruct the sleeping person softly, "You are now dreaming," once you have an indication that the person is dreaming.

In short, when the meditator perceives the clarity of
perceptive form and its unidentifiable emptiness as being
the inseparable, denuded union of appearance and emptiness
or emptiness and appearance, he has gained insight into
the intrinsic coemergence of appearance. The analogy of
a dream illustrates well this experience. Whatever diverse
forms a dreamer dreams, such as the material world, the
outer container, sentient beings, and the inner flavor, they
are nothing more than the functions of the dreamer's subtle
consciousness. So are the immediate appearances of dualistic
distortions, which arise out of the unobstructed vitality of
the mind's innate emptiness and continue to arise until the
meditator's common collective karma is purified.

When we've had some bad dream, as soon as we wake up, we tend to be unhappy and grouchy. The reason for our bad mood is that we grasp on to the contents of that bad dream as being real, and this allows its influence to continue throughout the day. Similarly, we feel cheerful upon waking up from a pleasant dream, and due to grasping on to that dream, we may remain in a good mood for the rest of the day. Whether the dreams are good or bad, there's no essence or reality to them.

While apprehending the dream-state, consider,
"Since this is now a dream-body, it can be transformed
in any way." Whatever arises in the dream, be it demonic
apparitions, monkeys, people, dogs, and so on, practice
multiplying them by emanation and changing them into
anything you like.

Morning's sun
loosens the hard ice;
so the sound of a staff
signals rescue by Jizo
from the cycle of rebirth.

When I used to visit Australian prisons to teach meditation, I would often hear the following prison proverb: "An extra hour of sleep is an hour off your sentence." People who don't like where they are will try to escape into dullness. In the same way, meditators who easily get negative will tend to drift into sloth and torpor. Ill will is the problem.

In addition to practicing during the waking state, if you can also use your consciousness during sleep for wholesome purposes, then the power of your spiritual practice will be all the greater. Otherwise at least a few hours each night will be just a waste. So if you can transform your sleep into something virtuous, this is useful. Try as you go to sleep to develop a wholesome mental state, such as compassion, or the realization of impermanence or emptiness.

If you can cultivate such wholesome mental states prior to sleep and allow them to continue right into sleep without getting distracted, then sleep itself becomes wholesome.

THE DALAI LAMA IN *SLEEPING, DREAMING, AND DYING*

There are five disadvantages to falling asleep thoughtlessly, without mindfulness: sleeping uneasily, waking unhappily, seeing a bad dream, not being guarded by gods, emitting impurity; five advantages come from mindfully falling asleep: sleeping easily, waking happily, not seeing a bad dream, being guarded by gods, not emitting impurity

When it is time to sleep, one should first wash one's feet and then lie down properly. One should lie on the right side of the body with the left leg on top of the right leg, which is called the lion posture and is the most beneficial position for the body and mind. When one is about to fall asleep, one should cultivate the thought of brightness; with skillful practice, even one's sleep and dreams will become bright. This way one will not be overly somnolent. Not only will one wake up easily, one will not dream; or if one dreams, the dreams will be free from afflictions and be about the Buddha, the Dharma, and the Sangha. When one is sleeping soundly, one has to maintain an alertness; one has to practice good deeds diligently even in one's sleep. Such a habit of sleeping is most useful for the recuperation of the body and mind. One's dreams will not become distorted, and one will not become lazy or desirous of sleep.

VENERABLE YIN-SHUN IN *THE WAY TO BUDDHAHOOD*

We have such a feeling of self-nature and cherish our "self" so much that even in sleep we think or dream of ourselves.

Sometimes when we're dreaming, when something very strange or frightening is taking place, part of ourselves, even while asleep, in the middle of the dream, manages to say, "I know I'm only dreaming; I can wake up at any time...." Our practice is like that, staying clear, staying present in the midst of our dream, in the midst of our daily life.

If we fall asleep full of joy and delight, then the odds are higher that when we wake up some of that feeling will resurface. This demonstrates something essential about the way the mind works, and we can put this knowledge to good use in our waking life. For instance, it can be very beneficial to intentionally sustain a sense of taking delight in others, and feeling kindly toward them—the emotions that we connect with having a noble frame of mind. For while that frame of mind is, of course, beneficial to others, it benefits ourselves as well.

Looking at the Moon

The moon was bright and I yearned for you so.
Smoothing my bedclothes, I went in the garden and
    gazed awhile
        at the moon.

Slowly, it became your face;
I could clearly see your broad brow, round nose,
    and fine mustache.
A year ago, I thought your face was like the moon;
Tonight the moon has become your face.

Since your face is the moon, so is mine.
But do you know that my face has become the waning
    moon?
Since your face is the moon, so is mine.

Upon recognizing the dream-state for what it is, you might bring forth the yearning to go to a pure realm; or you might simply view your present environment as already being a pure realm.

The only essential difference between waking and dreaming experiences is that the former arise with sensory input and the latter without it.

In Tantric Buddhism or Vajrayana, there are said to be four stages in the process of falling asleep, culminating in the so-called clear light of sleep. From that clear light of sleep, you arise into the dream state of REM sleep. A person untrained in meditation can't tell whether the four stages described in Vajrayana Buddhism are unalterable. However, a person who is well trained in Vajrayana meditation can recognize a strict order in these four states of falling asleep, and is well prepared to ascertain an analogous order in the dying process. It's easier to recognize the dream as the dream than to recognize dreamless sleep as dreamless sleep. If you can recognize the dream state while in it, then you can visualize and deliberately reduce the grosser level of mind to return again to clear light sleep. At that point the subtlest level of mind—the clear light of sleep—is easier to ascertain. Going through this transition without blacking out is one of the highest accomplishments for a yogi. According to Vajrayana Buddhism, these four stages are said to repeat in reverse order when you awaken from the dream state. It happens very quickly.

The World-Honored One Gazes at the Shining Stars

Present, past, heaven and earth—no more rebirth,
So what need for special analysis and explication?
And yet now night after night shining stars appear;
Is it not perhaps a convocation of the compassionate?

Attention! Ungan asked Dogo, "What does the great compassionate bodhisattva do when she uses her manifold hands and eyes?" Dogo said, "It's like a man who reaches behind him at night to search for his pillow." Ungan said, "I understand." Dogo said, "What do you understand?" Ungan said, "All over the body are hands and eyes." Dogo said, "You've really said it—you got eighty percent of it." Ungan asked, "Elder brother, how about you?" Dogo replied, "Throughout the body are hands and eyes."

Trusting fate, I just spend my time. Morning after
morning, the sun rises in the east. Evening after evening,
the moon sets in the west. The clouds disperse and
mountain valleys are still. After the rain, the mountains in
the four directions are close. Every four years is a leap
year. A rooster crows toward sunrise.

The Buddha was here—is here still, embodied in the Dhamma that now shines around us steadier than the starlight.

Just as dream content is not thought to be different from the dreamer who creates it, so also appearances are not different from mind. They *are* the very mind as it emanates.

TASHI NAMGYEL QUOTED IN *POINTING OUT THE GREAT WAY*

Though while awake I am no longer who I was while asleep, I can recognize myself: I am not a cauliflower. Nonetheless, if I turn my wakeful gaze inward, the unidimensional coherence of my self begins to erode. Perhaps a cauliflower I may yet become.

Without the intention to awaken,
there can only be sleep.

EZRA BAYDA WITH JOSH BARTOK IN *SAYING YES TO LIFE*

During a dream, if one feels compassion,
it is genuine compassion that arises.

The rootless mind dreamed
A dream during the third part of the night;
This was the teacher who showed the identity
of dream-appearance with the mind.
Do you understand?

Always indeed he sleeps well,
The brahmin who is fully quenched,
Who does not cling to sensual pleasures,
Cool at heart, without acquisitions.

Having cut off all attachments,
Having removed care from the heart,
The peaceful one sleeps well,
Having attained peace of mind.

Integration with the clear light of the elements: At first, when you fall asleep with your forehead covered with warmth, earth is dissolving into water. At that time, train in the vivid sense of clarity and emptiness, and focus your interest at the heart. Then when consciousness sinks, water is dissolving into fire; and at that time do not lose the vivid sense of clarity and emptiness. When the mind becomes agitated, fire is dissolving into air; and at that time, too, train in the vivid sense of clarity and emptiness. Falling fast asleep corresponds to air dissolving into consciousness, and at that time, too, clearly and vividly focus on your heart, without losing the earlier sense of clarity and emptiness. Then the state of dreamless lucidity corresponds to the consciousness dissolving into the clear light, and at that time your sleep will lucidly remain in the clarity and emptiness that is unborn and devoid of recollection. If you recognize the clarity and emptiness of that occasion, which is free of the intellect, this is called "recognizing the clear light." That is similar to the dissolution of consciousness into the clear light at the time of death, so this is training for the intermediate state between death and rebirth. The present recognition of the dream-state is the real training for the intermediate state.

Just as the radiance of all the stars does not equal a sixteenth part of the moon's radiance, but the moon's radiance surpasses them and shines forth, bright and brilliant, even so, whatever grounds there are for making merit productive of a future birth, all these do not equal a sixteenth part of the liberation of mind by loving-kindness. The liberation of mind by loving-kindness surpasses them and shines forth, bright and brilliant.

Just as in the last month of the rainy season, in the autumn, when the sky is clear and free of clouds, the sun, on ascending, dispels the darkness of space and shines forth, bright and brilliant, even so, whatever grounds there are for making merit productive of a future birth, all these do not equal a sixteenth part of the liberation of mind by loving-kindness. The liberation of mind by loving-kindness surpasses them and shines forth, bright and brilliant.

And just as in the night, at the moment of dawn, the morning star shines forth, bright and brilliant, even so,

whatever grounds there are for making merit productive of a
future birth, all these do not equal a sixteenth part
of the liberation of mind by loving-kindness. The liberation
of mind by loving-kindness surpasses them and shines forth,
bright and brilliant.

My Dream

When you stroll in the tree shade in the fresh of dawn,
my dream becomes a small star keeping watch above you.

When you nap on a summer's day flushed with heat,
my dream becomes a refreshing breeze swirling around you.

When you sit in solitude reading on a quiet autumn night,
my dream becomes a cricket chirping under your desk.

As you go to bed at night, resolve to wake up and recall your dreams throughout the night. As soon as you awaken from the dream, try to recall as many details as possible from the dream, and when you are about to fall back asleep, focus your mind on the resolve, "The next time I dream, I shall recognize it as a dream!" And just before you doze off, imagine that you are back in the dream from which you just awakened.

Dreams are seen by ordinary people; those who have perfected themselves do not see dreams.

Most of the time, people fall asleep with their mind in an uncontrolled or even disturbed state. It is much better to maintain awareness while falling asleep than to do so distractedly. If you can meditate while in bed, this is extremely beneficial, since your entire sleep can then be transformed into Dharma wisdom. By concentrating your mind beforehand, you can assure yourself of a restful and beneficial sleep.

It turns out that naps are really good times to have lucid dreams.

In the dream-state the clear light of awareness will appear
like the essence of limpid space, clear and empty, free
of the intellect.

Describing the eleven virtues of loving kindness, the Buddha said: "One sleeps in comfort, wakes in comfort, and dreams no evil dreams."

Bassui said: "Do you have dreams?"

A questioner replied: "When in a dead sleep, I usually dream."

Bassui: "What do you usually see in your dreams?"

Questioner: "It's not always fixed, but I usually see things that occur in my mind and through my body."

Bassui: "The rising and sinking after death are also like that. All thoughts that occur in the mind come by way of the four elements that comprise this physical body. Dreams in the night follow suit and appear in accord with good and bad thoughts of the day. Depending on the severity of the three karmic activities of the body, mouth, and mind, you rise or sink after death. That's why an ancient said: 'You receive a body according to your karma, and your body in turn produces karma.' Here you should realize the continuity of the body in this life with the body in the next one. If you truly understand this, you cannot doubt the statement, 'The one spirit is this skin pouch; this skin pouch is the one spirit.'"

FROM *MUD AND WATER*

Tibetan Buddhism considers sleep to be a form of nourishment, like food, that restores and refreshes the body. Another type of nourishment is *samadhi,* or meditative concentration. If one becomes advanced enough in the practice of meditative concentration, then this itself sustains or nourishes the body.

THE DALAI LAMA IN *SLEEPING, DREAMING, AND DYING*

When we are dreaming, all kinds of mental processes continue, even though our bodies and physical senses are dormant. Our emotional responses to dreams are just as real, and have the same impact on the body and the breath, as our emotions when we are wide awake. The only break we have from such sensory and mental input is when we are in deep, dreamless sleep. It's then that the respiration can flow without disruptive influences from the mind. I believe this is the healthiest breathing that occurs for most of us throughout the day and night. At the end of the day, we may fall asleep exhausted, but then eight hours later, we wake up, fresh and ready for a new day. All too often, this turns out to be just one more day of throwing our bodies and minds out of balance.

We now have the opportunity to break this habit. We don't have to wait until we're asleep before respiration can heal the day's damage. With mindfulness of breathing, we can do it anytime. Not controlling the breath, we let the respiration flow as effortlessly as possible, allowing the body to restore its balance in its own way.

B. ALAN WALLACE IN *THE ATTENTION REVOLUTION*

When someone has a nightmare, that person suffers.
For the dreamer, the nightmare is real; in fact, it is the
only reality the dreamer knows. And yet the dream has no
tangible reality and is not actually "real"; it has no reality
outside of the dreamer's own conditioned mind, outside of
the dreamer's own karma. From an ultimate perspective, it
is in fact an illusion. The dreamer's illusion is in failing to
recognize the nature of his experiences. Ignorant of what
they actually are, the dreamer takes his own productions
—the creations of his own mind—to be an autonomous
reality; thus deluded, he is frightened by his own
projections and thereby creates suffering for himself.
The delusion is to perceive as real what actually is not.
Buddha Shakyamuni taught that all the realms of cyclic
or conditioned existence, all things, all our experiences
are, in general, illusory appearances that cannot be
considered as either truly real or completely illusory.

KALU RINPOCHE IN *LUMINOUS MIND*

When you lie down, you take note of the breath and when sleepiness arises, you just note, "sleepiness, sleepiness, sleepiness," and let sleep come to you.

A Dream Remembered

Sitting firmly on the plantain-leaf mat, I can
    meditate in peace,
Surrounded by golden lamps flickering by the
    Dharma seat.
Wise birds emerge singing from deep within
    the woodlands,
A confusion of mountains soars up and into
    my small window.
Clouds fuse with the deep blue seas to mold
    this glorious day,
The dew washes the empty heavens, scatters
    the morning mist.
I recall how in my dream, I had a meeting
    with my Buddha;
Form is emptiness, emptiness form: now I know
    what it means.

Dream yoga allows illusions to be purified by themselves.

Many people find the prospect of lucid dreaming daunting because they have a hard time recalling their dreams, or even when they do, the dreams themselves may be unclear and their recollection of them may be vague. These are problems of attentional laxity, which are directly remedied through the practice of *shamatha* (attentional stability). Another problem often encountered when first venturing into the practices of lucid dreaming is waking up as soon as you recognize that you are dreaming. Even if you don't wake up, the dream may fade out and your lucidity may go with it. Or the dream may continue, but you may lose your awareness that it is a dream. These problems stem from insufficient attentional stability, which shamatha is also designed to develop. So shamatha appears to be perfectly designed to provide you with just those qualities of attention needed to become adept at lucid dreaming.

Suppose someone asked me, Eihei, "What is this sutra?"
I would say to him: If you call it "this sutra," your eyebrows
will fall out from lying. As to "How should we receive and
maintain it?" I would say: Reaching back for your pillow in
the middle of the night.

In Arnhem Land a man named Maralung was sleeping. In a dream, a master songman came to him and said, "Wake up, I have a song to teach you." At first there was a *min-min* light approaching through the trees. But when the light approached it was a human being. The dreamer woke up within the dream and the master taught him the song. But then the dreamer went back to sleep and forgot the song. Next day, a musicologist asked him for the song. So the next night, Maralung dreamed again and it happened the same way. Again the master came into his dream and woke him and taught him the song, and again he fell asleep afterward. But in the morning he remembered the song. So, what is the song? Why do we go back to sleep and forget it again and again? And when you wake, knowing it at last, who wakes?

The reality of our everyday life
depends on shared
conditionality—

it is a common dream,
not a private one.

One Dutchman describes his excitement at realizing
lucidity for the first time: in the dream he runs up to
a taxi driver shouting, "I'm dreaming. This is all a
dream. You are part of my dream!" and the taxi driver,
understandably since he has been confronted by
a lunatic, rolls up the window and speeds away.

ROBERT LANGAN IN *MINDING WHAT MATTERS*

The wisdom of Zen is often reduced to "chop wood, carry water"—to simply do what we're doing without unnecessary thinking. But this can be more simplistic than wise.
To be immersed in what we're doing does not necessarily mean that we're awake. In fact, being absorbed in activity is often the deepest form of sleep. Being awake in activity means paying attention to the activity, but not in a narrow way, where most of life is shut out. Fully doing includes a broader awareness, with a larger sense of presence and clarity of mind.

With the understanding of the mind's abiding nature, the meditator seeks to consolidate his determinate awareness for a whole day at a time. Once this is achieved, he extends it to a night, until he is able to perfectly link his daytime and nighttime meditations.

DAKPO TASHI NAMGYAL IN *MAHAMUDRA—THE MOONLIGHT*

As complex mental events, dreams are not always easy to understand. From the perspective of mindful therapy, working with dreams is worthwhile, even when no fully satisfying interpretation is reached. From a mindfulness perspective, it is the awareness, the process of gentle attending, which heals, in dream work as elsewhere.

One one occasion a certain bhikkhu was dwelling among the Kosalans in a certain woodland thicket. Now on that occasion when that bhikkhu had gone for his day's abiding he fell asleep. Then the devata that inhabited that woodland thicket, having compassion for that bhikkhu, desiring his good, desiring to stir up a sense of urgency in him, approached him and addressed him in verses:

"Get up, bhikkhu, why lie down?
What need do you have for sleep?
What slumber [can there be] for one afflicted,
Stricken, pierced by the dart?

"Nurture in yourself that faith
With which you left behind the home life
And went forth into homelessness:
Don't come under sloth's control."

The bhikkhu:
"When he's free, detached among those bound,
When his knowledge has been cleansed,
When he is sorrowless, beyond despair,
Energetic and resolute,
Always firm in his exertion,
Aspiring to attain Nibbana,
Why trouble one gone forth?"

One of the obstacles of dreaming is *dispersal through forgetfulness:* This entails apprehending the dream-state, but immediately becoming confused and letting the dream go on as usual. To dispel that, train in the illusory body during the day, and accustom yourself to envisioning the dream-state. Then as you are about to go to sleep, do so with the yearning, "May I know the dream-state as the dream-state, and not become confused." Also cultivate mindfulness, thinking, "Also, when I am apprehending the dream-state, may I not become confused." That will dispel it.

If It's a Dream

If love's bondage is a dream,
then so is liberation from the world.
If laughter and tears are dreams,
then so is the illumination of no-mind.
If the laws of all creation are a dream,
then I'll attain immortality in the dream of love.

To gain the proper experience during sleep and the waking state, I think it is crucial to become familiar, by means of imagination, with the eightfold process of dying, beginning with the waking conscious state and culminating in the clear light of death. This entails a dissolution process, a withdrawal. At each stage of the actual dying process there are internal signs, and to familiarize yourself with these, you imagine them during meditation in your daytime practice. Then in your imagination, abiding at the clear light level of consciousness, you visualize your subtle body departing from your gross body, and you imagine going to different places; then finally you return and the subtle body becomes reabsorbed in your normal form. Once you are experienced at visualizing this during the daytime practice, then when you fall asleep an analogous eightfold process occurs naturally and quickly. That's the best method for enabling you to recognize the dreamless sleep state as the dreamless sleep state. But without deeper meditative experience of this in the daytime, it's very difficult to realize this dissolution as you fall asleep.

In *The Large Sutra on Perfect Wisdom,* Shariputra asks if
a bodhisattva can grow in wisdom while dreaming,
and Subhuti answers:

> If he grows throughout the development by day, then
> he also grows in a dream.

> And why? Because dream and waking are indiscriminate.
> If the bodhisattva who courses by day in the perfection of
> wisdom has a development of the perfection of wisdom,
> then also the bodhisattva who dreams will have a
> development of the perfection of wisdom.

SERINITY YOUNG IN *DREAMING IN THE LOTUS* | 119

You should check carefully to see what mental impressions are predominant as you await sleep. You may have been very conscious of your actions throughout the day, but if you go to sleep without examining your mind, you can waste whatever positive energy you have created.

LAMA YESHE AND LAMA ZOPA RINPOCHE IN WISDOM ENERGY

When we engage in purification practices, we can look
for signs that we are actually purifying unwholesome
impressions on our mindstreams. One of these is obvious:
the decrease or elimination of unwholesome behavior.
Signs of purification also manifest in dreams, such as dreams
of vomiting bad food, drinking milk or eating yogurt, seeing
the sun or moon, dreaming that one is flying or that one's
body is on fire. If any of these dreams occur repeatedly
in the course of spiritual practice, this suggests that one's
mindstream is being purified of unwholesome imprints.

The different births that the karmically conditioned mind can take are comparable to a series of dreams; the passage from one dream to the next is like a death at the end of each dream and a rebirth at the beginning of the next one. Karmic tendencies and imprints create one dream, then a second, then a third, until the moment of awakening, at which point the dream appearances disappear. Likewise, karma causes us to live out different births and deaths in samsara as long as enlightenment has not been realized.

KALU RINPOCHE IN *LUMINOUS MIND*

The term *buddha* literally means "one who is awake," and the implication here is that the rest of us are comparatively asleep, moving through life as if in a dream. When you're dreaming and don't know it, that's called a *nonlucid dream,* but when you recognize that you're dreaming in the midst of the dream, this is called a *lucid dream.* The overall aim of Buddhist insight practice is to "wake up" to all states of consciousness, both during the daytime and nighttime, to become lucid at all times.

According to Tibetan Buddhism, to be in the sleeping state presupposes that the mental factor of sleep has manifested, and sleep can occur with or without dreaming. But if dreaming occurs, the mental factor of sleep must be present. The mental factor of sleep is the basis for dreaming as well as dreamless sleep. In one text, a Tibetan scholar makes the almost contradictory statement that in deep sleep there is no sleep, because there is no awareness or consciousness. Thus, sleep, as one of the mental factors, is not present in deep sleep.

Lie down, lion-like. This means on your right side, placing one foot on the other, clearly aware of what you are doing and keeping in mind the thought of rising. You say, "I will wake up at such and such a time in the morning." So, when you want to wake up in the morning without an alarm, you make a decision, before you go to sleep, "I will wake up in the morning early." When you have something to do in the morning which is really important, you will wake up at the right time, because you have made up your mind that you will wake up at that time. You really do wake up at that time. "Keeping in mind the thought of rising" means making up your mind to wake up in the morning at a certain time. When waking up, you should get up quickly. No snooze alarm.

Not Sleeping

Long night, no inclination to sleep,
empty hall, opening and shutting doors:
deliberately I move out of the glow of the lamp,
wait where I'll catch the moonlight when it comes.
Falling leaves suspended, snagged in a bird's nest,
streams of fireflies circling round me—
at dawn I dust off the sutra stand,
sandalwood ash from one stick of incense.

According to Tibetan Buddhism, appearances in a dream arise from the substrate consciousness and vanish back into it.

Totally asleep at night, somehow your head slips off
the pillow and you grope around, trying to find it,
without thinking, without discrimination—like the
mother who unhesitatingly cuddles her crying child.
You don't care if the pillow has a satin pillowcase or
a coarse linen one; you embrace any and every pillow
without discrimination. In the same way, Avalokiteshvara
embraces every being without discrimination, with total
freedom of activity. Not limited by ideas of enlightenment or delusion, self or other, just embrace that pillow.

GERRY SHISHIN WICK IN *THE BOOK OF EQUANIMITY*

Even if awakened, the cold wind blows and chills me, and I don't yet know for whom the bright moon is white. This is a saying of practice together. How do you speak a statement that transcends Dharma and goes beyond marrow, that is without high, middling, and lowly, and that expresses the utmost heights? Still, do you thoroughly understand? A white heron stands in the snow, but they are not the same color. The bright moon shines on the white reed flowers, but one does not resemble the other.

In order to achieve the ultimate states of Dharmakaya, Sambhogakaya, and Nirmanakaya, one must become acquainted with the three stages of death, intermediate state, and rebirth. In order to become acquainted with these three, one must gain acquaintance with the states of dreamless sleep, dreaming, and waking.

As the gray darkens in the east, stars appear, and the immensity of the universe becomes once again visible [...] How might we acquire a faith that actually comforts and inspires us who are mortal and temporary?

What constitutes a frame of mind, be it waking or
dreaming, is an *enframing* reality. The insomniac and
the dreamer both move in realms of the real. Reality for
the one comprises tousled sheets and the unrelenting
concerns of the day; for the other, who knows? The
dream is real in its own terms, in its own spewing stream
of consciousness, a world unto itself. That world may
seem less predictable than the waking world, until one
reflects, uneasily, that even awake one never really knows
what happens next. Normal dreaming enfolds the
dreamer in a reality of the night, day mind forgotten.
When a nightmare scares one out of one's wits, one finds
oneself, witlessly, awake. New reality: day mind to the
rescue. Where is the crossover, the point between?

ROBERT LANGAN IN *MINDING WHAT MATTERS*

Lie in bed deeply relaxed but vigilant, and perform
a repetitive or continuous mental activity upon which
you focus your attention. Keeping this task going is
what maintains your inner focus of attention and with it
your wakeful inner consciousness, while your drowsy
external awareness diminishes and finally vanishes
altogether as you fall asleep. In essence, the idea is to let
your body fall asleep while you keep your mind awake.

Thinking you finally understand awakening will lull you into the deepest sleep of all.

In nightly meditation one should reproach oneself
For each uncontrolled deed of the day;
Each day one should reproach oneself for any evil deed
   committed at night.
Having done so properly one should rejoice.

And how, friend, is one devoted to wakefulness?
Here, during the day, while walking back and forth
and sitting, a bhikkhu purifies his mind of obstructive
states. In the first watch of the night, while walking
back and forth and sitting, he purifies his mind of
obstructive states. In the middle watch of the night
he lies down on his right side in the lion's posture with
one foot overlapping the other, mindful and clearly
comprehending, after noting in his mind the idea
of rising. After rising, in the last watch of the night,
while walking back and forth and sitting, he purifies
his mind of obstructive states. It is in this way, friend,
that one is devoted to wakefulness.

When you enter the state that is unborn and devoid of recollection, you do not remember anything and you are without thoughts of any kind. This training of realizing the clear light during the sleeping process is a preparation for being able to recognize the clear light during the dying process. This is like boot camp, in which soldiers are very thoroughly exercised and trained for the occasion when they actually meet with the enemy.

In the "sleeping-lion posture," you lie on your right side, with your right hand beneath your right cheek and your left hand resting on your left thigh. This is the position in which the Buddha reportedly passed away, and it has been strongly recommended ever since as a suitable posture in which to sleep mindfully.

Running parallel to beliefs and practices concerning the dream state is the understanding that even in the waking state we are all asleep, that is, unenlightened—dreaming our life away while immersed in illusion. We need to wake up, to recognize what is real and proceed toward the ultimate awakening, enlightenment.

A Beautiful Memory

In a tower brushed by the wind of the Inland Sea,
My teacher and I share an evening.
When I awake I am alone in the Western Hemisphere.
More than seventy years have I been dreaming,
While on the Alaya Sea floats the illusionary boat.

Many times, after a particularly stimulating day, you may think, "I just can't fall asleep. What can I do?" The mind is tossed in so many directions by the day's energy still echoing in your brain that sleep is impossible. Meditation can focus your mind when it is in such an agitated state, and calm it so that you can go to sleep. Some of you already know that this is true from your own experience: Even during the day how many times have you fallen asleep while meditating?

While dreaming, we have the sense of having a body, we observe other people and our environment, and we may experience all types of emotions. We can move from one place to another simply by a shift of consciousness. Such travel is not limited even by the speed of light. It is instantaneous. We think of a place and we are there, simultaneous with our thinking. Similarly, in the bardo state, one has a body that is made of the stuff that dreams are made on: it is purely a mental body, a creation of the mind. This mental body is replete with sense faculties, and with it one can observe other people and events in the bardo. As in the dream state, one can move as swiftly as thought, and one's vision is unimpeded, that is, where one looks, one sees.

B. ALAN WALLACE IN *TIBETAN BUDDHISM FROM THE GROUND UP*

All evil thoughts are born of deluded feelings. If you do not see penetratingly into your own nature, though you try to eliminate evil thought you will be like one who tries to stop dreaming without waking from his sleep.

In a clear dream, our dream body acts; it sees forms, hears sounds, and experiences an imaginary world in exactly the same way our present body experiences the world we know in our waking state. When we awaken, the dream body disappears, but the mind continues to experience with another body, our physical body, in another world— that of our waking state. The phenomenon of death is similar to this, only this time it is our physical body— the body of our waking state—that disappears.

During the hypnagogic state of consciousness—a deep state of relaxation as we fall asleep, with our minds withdrawn from the physical senses—there can be a high degree of vividness. I suspect that the exceptional vividness of this transitional phase of consciousness and of some dreams may be due in part to the fact that the mind is relaxed and disengaged from the senses, so there is little competition from other stimuli. But dreams are not usually stable, and we normally have little control in them. That is why the sequence of *shamatha* (mental balance and attention) training begins with relaxation, then stabilizing attention, and finally maintaining relaxation and stability while gradually increasing vividness.

I don't know how late the night is.
The heavy shadows over Mount Sörak are thinning.
As I wait for the dawn bell, I lay down my brush.

One of the obstacles of dreaming is *dispersal through waking:*
As soon as novices recognize, "This is a dream!" they wake
up and there is dispersal of that recognition. (This is a
problem of overexertion, practicing so forcefully that the
very recognition of the dream-state bolts one out of sleep.)
To dispel that, maintain your attention at the level of the
heart and below, and focus your mind on a black bindu the
size of a pea, called the "syllable of darkness," on the soles
of both feet. That will dispel it.

Try to see the first moment of waking up. As soon as you wake up, say, "I am waking up, waking up, waking up." In waking up, you also apply clear comprehension.

VENERABLE U SILANANDA IN *THE FOUR FOUNDATIONS OF MINDFULNESS*

In Buddhism, the origin of dreams is understood as an interface between different degrees of subtlety of bodies—the gross level, the subtle level, and the very subtle level. But if you ask why we dream, what's the benefit, there's no answer in Buddhism.

Drop off the body: the river of the world will never end,
Stately and grand: nothing to show by the inner master.
When morning comes, change the water, light the
   incense,
Everything is in the ordinary affairs of the everyday
   world.

If we go out on a clear night and gaze up at the stars, we can see stars hundreds of light-years away. We gaze out there and see a tiny white dot, but the star as we perceive it is dependent upon the visual faculties with which we are seeing it. The perceived star would not exist without someone to see it. Is the star that we perceive out there, many light-years away, or is it somewhere else? The idea that it is out there is obviously absurd, for it would imply that our eyes are able to condition something hundreds of light-years away.

To make it more absurd, the star is not there where we see it anyway. The star has moved since its light started journeying across space hundreds of years ago, and the place where we see the star may be nothing but empty space.

Although the true Dharma eye treasury, wondrous mind of nirvana, is what buddhas protect and keep in mind, it cannot be defiled by the Buddha Dharma. Although it was correctly transmitted by arhats, the true Dharma eye treasury did not descend into the dharma of shravakas. Although it was correctly transmitted by common people, it did not descend into the dharma of sentient beings. If this were not true, how could it have ever reached us now? Great assembly, do you want to clearly know the key to why this is so?

After a pause Dogen said: After midnight the moon sets and the nest is chilled with night. The thousand-year-old crane does not remain in the jewel forest.

I remember once watching a dog asleep in the middle of a party. At the feet of all the tensely talking and drinking adults, she lay in deep self-abandon, her paws in the air, a beatific smile on her face, fully at home in the world. We were edgily being at a party; she was a full member of the celebration, of being alive in a body.

If you have arrived at the point where you can recognize dreamless sleep as dreamless sleep, then it's very easy for you to recognize the dream as the dream.

THE DALAI LAMA IN *SLEEPING, DREAMING, AND DYING*

Enlightenment is the realization of the unity and harmony of ourselves and externals. It is the way of awakening from a bad dream in which we separate ourselves from everything and everybody, creating all kinds of problems and difficulties.

The "I" who appears in the dream is not synonymous with the "I" who is dreaming; the "I" who knows both sways somewhere between. The dangling "I" is open, being both "I's" and neither, like a word repeated after itself so often that it starts to become a strange sound, divorced from meaning.

Those who place their faith in sleep
Will procrastinate and fall further into slumber.

A major cause of forgetting dreams is interference from other mental contents competing for your attention, so let the first thought upon awakening be "What was I just dreaming?" Just as movement disrupts attentional stability while meditating, it also undermines the coherence and continuity of dreaming, so do not move when you first wake up. Redirect your attention to the dream from which you just awoke, and see if you can slip right back into it, mindfully aware that it is a dream.

B. ALAN WALLACE IN *THE ATTENTION REVOLUTION*

The new moon may be incomplete in its form, yet it is still the moon.

According to the Abhidharma texts, sleep is seen as virtuous, non-virtuous, or neutral depending on the immediately preceding consciousness—the mind just prior to sleep. That mind makes a huge difference to the mind of sleep. If the mind before sleep is virtuous, such as the thought that we will sleep not just to rest but to refresh the body in order to have energy to help ourselves and others, then our sleeping mind will more likely be virtuous. Similarly, if we fall asleep with a mind wholly bent on liberation, that is a wonderful way to ensure that our entire sleeping time is very positive, no matter how long we sleep. For those of us who love to sleep, perhaps this is the best practice!

The key to listening to another's dreams is to keep that
person working and processing, rather than putting
yourself in the position of needing to have all the answers.
The simple device of asking that person to describe a
common object such as a cat, a dog, a chair, a house, and so
forth, as though attempting to tell someone from another
planet what these things are, can often yield surprising
insight.

When you no longer are asleep,
All dreams will vanish by themselves.
If mind does not discriminate,
All things are as they are, as One.
To go to this mysterious source
Frees us from all entanglements.

Most of us assume that we are lucid—clearly aware of
the nature of our existence—while in the waking state,
but in comparison to a buddha, we are sleepwalkers, moving
through life and death in a nonlucid dream. According
to the Dzogchen view, everything in the entire universe
consists of phenomena arising from the primordial unity
of pristine awareness and the absolute space of phenomena.
If we viewed reality from that perspective, instead of from
the limited vantage point of a human psyche, the whole
world would appear as a dream, and we would be the
dreamer. The potentials of freedom for those who are
truly awakened are infinite.

Lucid dreamers are often people who are willing to take internal risks.

When the dreamer is in the city of dream he should hold
both pleasure and sorrow as mere thought, as being like
appearances reflected in a mirror, as neither existent nor
non-existent, nor both existent and non-existent, as like
a rainbow in the sky, or the sound of thunder, or perceiving
being born and ceasing. The person who remains in clarity
understands that all things are like this.

While dreaming, you should remember that everything that happens is no more substantial than a dream. There is really no jumper into a raging torrent; there is no jumping; there's no water to jump into. With that realization, you jump into the river. This practice is not only to be applied to jumping into a river, but to any dangerous situation involving any of the four elements. In the dream-state, you could encounter a dangerous animal or any other fearful circumstance, including finding that you're in a hot hell, a cold hell, and so on. Therefore, in any fearful situation recognize your own state as simply a mental body, and recognize every aspect of the dream as nothing more than a dream. With this awareness, enter into what ostensibly looks like a dangerous situation. I hasten to emphasize that this is a dream practice. Don't think that you can go to the Golden Gate Bridge and jump off, thinking, "Well, there is no real jumper," because you will terminate your life and create problems for yourself for at least five hundred lifetimes thereafter.

Moreover, in this dream-state, if you practice correctly, you'll be carried away by a current of bliss and emptiness— which will not likely happen if you jump off the Golden Gate Bridge.

One of the reasons it is necessary to go to sleep peacefully is that the dream state is much more powerful and effective than the waking one. The reason I say this is that although you may think you are paying exclusive attention to something while awake, your other senses are still open and they respond to the conflicting impressions they receive. During your dreams, however, the five physical senses—seeing, hearing, smelling, tasting, and touching—are not active. When you see something in a dream, for instance, you do so with your mind's eye, not your physical one. In the absence of such sensory distractions, then, your mind is left naturally concentrated with great energy. Thus, the effect of dreaming about greed, for instance, can be much stronger and leave a deeper imprint on your mind than when a stray thought of attachment arises in your heart during the day. And, of course, the same holds true if in your dreams you can focus on an aspect of the spiritual path.

According to the Buddhist theory of the conservation of
mental events, some forms of consciousness are manifest,
while others are latent. For example, when you are angry
about something the mental event of anger is manifest,
but when you become calm again, the anger becomes latent.
When you witness a beautiful sunset, your awareness of it is
manifest, but afterward that awareness becomes latent. In
the dream state both the waking consciousness (including
sensory awareness) and the consciousness of
deep sleep are latent; in the waking state dreaming
awareness and deep sleep are dormant; and while in deep
sleep, the dreaming and waking consciousness are latent.

The clear light of sleep occurs, I believe, as you're falling asleep. It manifests during the interval after all of the daytime appearances have vanished and just before any dream appearances arise. Similarly, the clear light momentarily manifests when you're on the verge of waking up after the appearances of the dream-state have passed and just before the appearances of the waking state arise—when some of the power of the daytime appearances is beginning to arise but the actual appearances have not yet arisen.

GYATRUL RINPOCHE IN *NATURAL LIBERATION*

A dream object is an external object affecting a mental consciousness just as a reflection in a mirror is an external object affecting an eye consciousness.

In general, around us there are many mysteries, many facts, that are not seen with the eye. Because we have a coarse physical body, when it is very active, it is difficult to have direct contact with these mysteries, but when we become semi-conscious—when our consciousness becomes more subtle—there is a diminishment of the coarse consciousnesses that depend on the coarse physical body, and it is easier to make a connection with such mysteries.

All of this I cried loudly in my sleep.
My lover's smile is like starlight, unvanquished by the rays
of blackness.
Before I knew it, the tears that racked my dreams had wet
my pillow.
Forgive me, my love.
It's the fault of dreaming, but if you want to punish, don't
punish dreams.

Like a dream, the world of waking experience does not exist independently of our experience of it. The daytime practices in preparation for lucid nighttime dreaming may help begin to wake you up to the nature of your experienced world. The most effective method of learning to achieve lucidity is to develop a "critical-reflective attitude" toward your state of consciousness by asking yourself whether or not you are dreaming while you are awake.

B. ALAN WALLACE IN *THE ATTENTION REVOLUTION*

Night Sitting

The hermit doesn't sleep at night:
in love with the blue of the vacant moon.
The cool of the breeze
that rustles the trees
rustles him too.

There are many different levels of subtlety in the clear light experience. For example, the clear light of sleep is not as deep as the clear light of death. In the clear light of sleep, the grosser forms of these various energies dissolve, or withdraw, but the subtle forms do not.

Just when wondering
If I would again see it
In this fall—
Under tonight's full moon
How can I sleep?

By closely attending to everything that arises with discerning mindfulness, you will gain a clearer and clearer awareness of the nature of waking reality, and that, in turn, can lead to lucidity in your dreams.

B. ALAN WALLACE IN *THE ATTENTION REVOLUTION*

At first glance it may seem strange even to think of putting dream together with the urgent matter of waking up in our life, but "dream," or *yume,* is a character often displayed on the walls of a Zen temple, a matter accorded deep respect and even gratitude.

When we sleep, let us sleep, but when we wake—as now, mindfully turning the page of a book in this day in this universe—there is the work of the wakeful to accomplish.

If your sleep is too deep, your dreams will not be very clear.
In order to bring about clearer dreams and lighter sleep,
you should eat somewhat less. In addition, as you're falling
asleep, you direct your awareness up to the forehead.
On the other hand, if your sleep is too light, this will also
act as an obstacle for gaining success in this practice.
In order to deepen your sleep, you should take heavier,
oilier food; and as you're falling asleep, you should direct
your attention down to the vital energy center at the level
of navel or the genitals. If your dreams are not clear, as
you're falling asleep you should direct your awareness
to the throat center.

Awake, I remember the dream, shiver at the nightmare, but however cinematically vivid it may be, the dream has become an image in my mind, a memory, safely this side of that curious, mysterious point of the between when image becomes reality, or reality, image.

If life has many adversities and is more transient
than even water bubbles blown by the wind,
amazing indeed it is that we inhale after exhaling
and wake up after going to sleep.

What is meant by the removal of ignorance? Imagine that you are dreaming and in your dream you drive somewhere, get into a bad accident, and are seriously injured. What do you really need to get rid of this pain and suffering? No amount of medical treatment or vehicle repair will actually help this situation, because the whole time you are safely asleep in your bed. The only remedy that will actually get rid of your suffering is the recognition that you are just dreaming and no accident has occurred. As soon as you realize this, your suffering will disappear.

From a mindfulness perspective, working with the dream to enlarge awareness is more important than reaching any neat or final interpretation.

One of the obstacles of dreaming is *dispersal through insomnia:* If sleep is dispersed due to powerful anticipation, and you become diffused as your consciousness simply does not go to sleep, counteract this by imagining a black *bindu* in the center of your heart. Bring forth the anticipation without force and just for an instant, and by releasing your awareness, without meditating on sleep, you will fall asleep and apprehend the dream-state.

PADMASAMBHAVA IN *NATURAL LIBERATION*

Another very effective way to become proficient in lucid dreaming is to wake up one hour earlier than usual, and stay awake for thirty to sixty minutes before going back to sleep. This can increase the likelihood of having a lucid dream by as much as twenty times. As you become more and more adept at maintaining the stability and vividness of your attention at all times, during and between meditation sessions, while awake and asleep, you will gain deeper and deeper insight into the nature of awareness.

At a retreat I led in Sydney a few years ago, a retreatant arrived late from her high-stress job as an executive in the city. In her first sitting that evening her mind was almost as dead as a corpse. So I gave her my special teaching on how to overcome her sloth and torpor: I told her to rest. For the next three days she slept in until dawn, went back to bed again after breakfast, and had a long nap after lunch. What a brilliant meditator!

The dream is both a personal and collective experience, both an immanent and a transcendent phenomenon.

After the night

She is afraid shadows will reveal indignities she has escaped
as light evades her room. That sorcerers will lift their skirts
and send thoughts to stick to her like damp leaves. She
gathers her belongings before sleep, thinking this will be
the night to explain matters of the past. It is rarely fear we
leave behind in childhood. A paper barely holding her
name and address, just in case; this she puts near her pillow
night after night. The fear of the resolute; like armies
marching into a blind night singing love songs.
She wonders if protection comes from prayers.
In the morning she laughs, calls herself a silly thing and the
night is forgotten. Or accepted as an advantage. Far away
in the future of her tongue are promises of condiments.
Turmeric. Saffron. Of nights irresponsible as statues in the
bazaar. These are pledged. Surely we can live again and
again through the same lesson. In her dream comes a
mother who has lost her street address. She speaks no
English and holds a key.

In the Tibetan tradition, dreams during pregnancy may carry import regarding the health and personality of the baby. In many cases, mothers will report a significant dream during pregnancy. However, it is often difficult to interpret or determine whether these dreams are truly connected to the baby. Many dreams are considered to have links to the unborn child. People say that if a child is destined to have a good life, the parents, especially the mother, will frequently have auspicious dreams in the latter part of the night, and the mother will experience a newfound joy.

ANNE HUBBELL MAIDEN AND EDIE FARWELL IN
THE TIBETAN ART OF PARENTING

During the entire dreaming process, even the subjects—
we who are dreaming—have no real existence.

During a dream, your physical body remains lying in your bed, but your dream body moves around, doing all sorts of things. It feels as if you have a body, but you don't. That is the same type of body that the mind has while moving around in the *bardo* of becoming. Therefore, you may not immediately realize that you have passed away.

Dreams that occur in the last part of the night around dawn are considered to have more meaning than those earlier in the night, which are often too greatly influenced by the previous day's activities to indicate deep predilections.

THE DALAI LAMA IN *KALACHAKRA TANTRA*

Lonely Night

No moon in the sky, no breeze on the ground,
no sound of people—and I, empty of mind.

Is the universe death?
Is life sleep?

The golden thread of love's memory attaches to my brow
    at one end;
to a little star at the other; and gently, gently disappears.
One hand grasps a golden sword, the other plucks celestial
    flowers,
and the queen of illusion also vanishes.
Who knew that love's golden thread and illusion's queen
would clasp hands, and, in tears, die for each other?

Is the universe death?
Is life tears?

If life is tears,
is death love?

MANHAE IN *EVERYTHING YEARNED FOR*   195

We speak of different embodiments of a buddha, including the Sambhogakaya, the very subtle body of an awakened being, and the Dharmakaya, the enlightened body of an awakened being. The practice of developing the special dream body is ultimately aimed at achieving the Sambhogakaya, whereas the ultimate purpose of ascertaining the clear light of death is achieving the Dharmakaya. The Sambhogakaya is an illusory body, or physical form in which a buddha appears to others, while the Dharmakaya is self-referential, directly accessible only to a buddha. So the practice of dream yoga relates to the Sambhogakaya, and the practice of the clear light of sleep relates to the Dharmakaya.

Tibetan texts say that dreams can be carried on the internal winds of the body and that these winds can be clarified and controlled through ascetic practices such as breath control and meditation. These practices also clarify consciousness: they give rise to a pure consciousness that is able to break free of physical and emotional limitations.

In spring I spend the day
with flowers, wanting no night;
it's turned around
in fall, when I watch the moon
all night, resenting the day.

When tired we sleep; when lively we practice zazen.

A *state check* enables you to determine whether, right now, you are awake or dreaming. During the waking state, the physical world you experience is not entirely dependent on your own mind. For example, as you read the pages of this book, although the visual images you are seeing are produced by your brain, the paper and ink were produced by other people and consist of chemical substances that do not depend for their existence on your perception of them. If you momentarily turn your head away from the book, the paper and ink still exist, although your visual perceptions of them don't. Given the independent status of the book relative to your perception of it, every time you look back to the lines of text on this page, you see the same words. On the other hand, if you were dreaming right now, the book you are reading would have no existence apart from your perception of it. It would be purely a creation of your own mind, so if you momentarily close your eyes or turn your head away, that dreamed book wouldn't exist at all. Being out of sight, it would be out of mind and cease to exist. Given the lack of continuity of any objective book in a dream, when you redirect your gaze back to the book, the words change seventy-five percent of the time if you reread it once, and ninety-five percent of the time if you reread it twice.

So try this right now. Turn your head away for a few seconds, then look at this page again. If the words change (and of course you would need to remember what they were previously to know that), then you are almost certainly dreaming. If they remain the same, you are probably awake. If you do this a second and even a third time, and the words still remain the same, then you can conclude with greater and greater certainty that you are not dreaming. But if they change even once, then you are probably correct to conclude that you are dreaming.

Chuang Tzu's famous story tells of a person who lay down in a field of grass under a gentle sun and fell into a dream of being a butterfly flitting from stem to stem of the warm, grassy field. Waking up, the sleeper could not say if he were a butterfly waking into the dream of being human, or a human being waking from a dream of being a butterfly.

SUSAN MURPHY IN *UPSIDE-DOWN ZEN*

For once, no words, no ideas occur to us. We listen and hear nothing, as the night flows cold over our limbs. The snow in the dim light near the steps is full of tracks turning here and there and round about forever. Slowly we step back and slowly we close the door. It is time to sleep.

Lucid dreaming reflects a human capacity to become experientially enmeshed in the complexity of a reality, while at the same time to transcend that reality.

The capacity may serve merely to bring back memorabilia, like snapshots from the dreamworld that can gather dust on the familiar mantle of my waking day.

Or the capacity may go further. In view of that turnabout point between realities, like the subtle point between inhalation and exhalation when neither in nor out applies, lucidity may go both ways. The dusty mantle might start to shimmer. Lucid dreaming is one crossover. Cross back, and its counterpart is lucid waking.

Throughout the course of the day, recall that tonight you will sleep and dream, and repeatedly arouse the strong resolution, "Tonight when I'm dreaming, I will recognize the dream state for what it is." The stability and vividness of attention that you have cultivated in your attention practice should serve you well now and bring clarity to all your experiences, both waking and dreaming.

Even in bed before falling asleep, think "I will take upon myself all the sufferings of sentient beings and their origins; I will give them my body, material resources— everything—and will help them all attain buddhahood." Because of this, all your sleeping moments will become the mind exchanging self and others.

KÖNCHOCK GYALTSEN IN *MIND TRAINING*

If we wake from sleep, the dream will dissolve and
we will experience the relief of being safe in the bed
of our true nature.

The rootless mind dreamed
A dream during the third part of the night;
This was the teacher who showed the identity
of dream-appearance with the mind.
Do you understand?

Dreaming is being awake, and being awake is a dream. Do not look upon dreams and your waking hours as separate. If you think that dreams and your waking hours are different, you cannot know the deeper place.

When contemplatives who are adept at dream yoga enter
into a lucid dream, they can have the satisfaction of
knowing that everything in their experience consists
of just the kinds of phenomena they wish to study:
they all consist of consciousness.

B. ALAN WALLACE IN *THE ATTENTION REVOLUTION*

In the *Satipatthana Sutta* one is asked to practice mindfulness focused on sleeping. Even arahants are not aware when they're asleep, so what does this mean? Some translators have attempted to solve this question by changing the meaning of the exercise to mindfulness on falling asleep. However, the Pali word used in the *Satipatthana Sutta* means "in sleep," and there is a different phrase for falling asleep, *niddam okkamati*. The practice of mindfulness focused on sleeping means one uses a previous experience of having been asleep as the focus of superpowered mindfulness in the present. It is mindfulness that takes an old experience as its object.

There are a lot of people who mix up their sleep with meditation—but not quite intentionally.

Buddhaghosa (the fifth-century Indian Buddhist commentator), for one, limits pure prophetic dreams to very special people, like the Buddha, his mother, and the king of Kosala, thereby creating a dreaming elite similar to that found in many other ancient cultures. The idea is that not just anyone's dream is meaningful. Prophetic dreams come to people who have accrued merit, either in a past or in their present life.

Engaging right now in an exercise to determine whether you are dreaming may seem silly since you presumably were already quite confident that you weren't dreaming. But we commonly have that same confidence when we *are* dreaming. We take what we experience in the world around us to be objectively real, existing independently of our awareness of it, and we respond to events as if we were awake. By conducting a *state check* intermittently throughout the course of the day, you can determine whether you are awake or asleep. And as you familiarize yourself with this practice, this habit may carry over into your dream state, and when you apply it then, you will suddenly discover that you *are* dreaming. This is how you begin to dream lucidly.

Poem Just Jotted Down

In the middle of the night,
I suddenly rise;

draw water
from the deep well.

White dew
covers the woods;

morning stars
dot the clear sky.

Always and everywhere, humans have faced two major life passages in which our habitual mind seems to dissolve and enter a radically different realm. The first passage is sleep, humanity's constant companion, transitory and filled with the dream life that has enchanted cultures from the beginning of history. The second is death, the grand and gaping enigma, the final event that organizes so much of individual existence and cultural ritual. These are ego's shadow zones, where Western science is often ill at ease, far from its familiar territory of the physical universe or physiological causality. In contrast, Tibetan Buddhist tradition is fully at home here; in fact, it has accumulated remarkable knowledge in this area.

The following practice, which is written in beautiful metered verse in Tibetan, would commonly be recited in the monasteries in Tibet. When I was a young boy, early in the morning monks would come around chanting this. It was a way to prevent people from sleeping in:

> *Without succumbing to the influence of ignorance and*
> *delusion,*
> *Bring forth the power of enthusiasm and get up now!*
> *From beginningless time until now*
> *You may have remained fast asleep due to ignorance,*
> *But now do not sleep; apply your body, speech, and mind*
> *to the Dharma.*

CHÖKYI NYIMA RINPOCHE AND DAVID R. SHLIM IN *MEDICINE & COMPASSION*

When we wake up in the morning, we should try our best to make the first thought that comes to mind a noble one—a very sincere and strong thought of doing good. We should make our first thought of the morning into a true desire to be of benefit to other beings. Then the momentum created by that positive intention can be with us for the rest of the day.

Even good dreams do not exist by way of their own nature and should not become objects of attachment by our assenting to their seeming inherent existence. Bad dreams, being without inherent existence, can be transformed and thus need not be seen as discouraging.

Waking from a Dream

If it's you, you would love me,
but is it love to come to my door every night then go,
    leaving only the sound of footsteps?
My footsteps have never been outside your door.
Maybe only you can love?
If your footsteps hadn't awakened me
I would be riding a cloud seeking you.

Individual dreamsigns consist of activities, situations, people, objects, and mental states that you commonly experience in your dreams. In order to identify and watch for these dreamsigns, you will need to pay close attention to your dreams and keep a dream journal, noting the circumstances that are recurrent. Remember these and whenever you experience them, pause for a moment and conduct a state check to see if you might be dreaming.

Another sense of dream is *mara*, in traditional Buddhism the delusory half-sleep that can steal our lives even while we dream we are awake and aware. We all know about that sleep that can steal whole seasons of our lives, and long to wake from it into something more alive. But this valuable cautionary and salutary sense of "dream" leaves out and attempts to leave behind much of the complexity and poetry of human experience; and it does not reach far enough into the true nature of that waking up experience. It may also encourage us to think of working hard to attain some pure condition of awakening in which such dark dreams as anger, fear, envy, grief, or regret may no longer have any relationship to us. That pure condition is itself a dream, and beneath its bright mirror, self-deception can lengthen in the shadows, undisturbed. It may seem a lovely dream, but it is a dream nonetheless. To confine yourself to dream as mara is to miss the deeper grounds for the obvious respect and gratitude in which Zen holds the matter of "dream."

SUSAN MURPHY IN *UPSIDE-DOWN ZEN*

So you should view the fleeting world:
A star at dawn, a bubble in the stream,
A flash of lightning in a summer cloud,
A flickering lamp, a phantom, and a dream.

FROM *THE DIAMOND SUTRA* 223

Nature is always piling its incidents upon our unreadiness. Hardly have we covered ourselves in blankets and turned a last, marveling gaze toward the window, when it is morning again. The fire is dead, and the room is brightening with natural light, and we are planting our feet on the cold floor and getting up into the whirl of samsara once again. Now then, where were we meaning to go? Shall it be a day to honor the Dhamma?

BHIKKHU NYANASOBHANO IN *AVAILABLE TRUTH*

Lucidity, then, is not an aspect of waking consciousness exported to the dream-state. Nor is it an aspect of dreaming consciousness leached into waking reality. While awake or dreaming or in some other frame of mind, lucidity becomes an awareness of the relative betweenness of experienced reality. Lucidity finds, and transcends, the frame. Lucid waking becomes another metaphor for enlightenment. Reality is real, all right, but not the whole picture. Any one reality seems to account for everything, but does so in its own self-limiting and self-defining terms.

In my dream I saw
the spring wind gently shaking
blossoms from a tree;
and even now, though I'm awake,
there's motion, trembling in my chest.

If you at any time experience an exceptionally odd situation, pause and ask yourself, "How odd is it?" While dreaming, we experience many anomalies, such as abrupt transitions of our location and other kinds of discontinuities, such as the words in a book changing, or other weird occurrences and circumstances. But without adopting a "critical-reflective attitude" toward them, we take them in stride, without waking up to the fact that we are dreaming. Adopt such a critical stance at all times, questioning the nature of your present experience; this habit, too, may carry over into the dream state and help you to become lucid.

When going to bed at night, cultivate the following thought: "Isn't it amazing that there are people like me who waste their precious human existence and bring harm upon themselves!" Thinking thus, appeal for forbearance, declare and purify your negative karma, and cultivate the resolve to forsake this in the future.

Imagine that a person is lying asleep in bed and dreaming. Beside the sleeping person is a second person with clair- voyance, who is awake and fully aware of the content of the other person's dreams. The person with extrasensory perception knows that the person who is asleep is just asleep in bed and what that person is experiencing is just dreams. In the same way, a buddha personally does not experience ignorance or confusion but does see the ignorance of beings in all its detail and variety.

Tibetan monks would rise at two or three in the morning when in retreat; but in hot countries it is difficult to do without sleep and also, you are not used to this kind of discipline. If you get up too early, you will get tired very easily and that will spoil your meditation. You should keep healthy and do your sleeping in bed, not on your meditation cushion. Whatever you do, do well.

From *Song of the Twelve Hours of the Day*

The sun sets—the tenth hour
A curve of the moon hangs over the willow by the window.
I blow on the kindling, and the furnace fills with smoke.
Four or five flecks of dark ash fly up over my head.

Golden dusk— the eleventh hour
Time for the mice to venture out to steal the pale honey.
At the foot of my bed they make a racket late into the night,
Which disturbs this mountain monk so she cannot sleep.

Everyone settled—the twelfth hour
The mustard seed drinks dry the Fragrant-Water Sea.
Beneath my robes, the *mani* jewel suddenly radiates light,
Singing in unison with the lanterns on the outside pillars.

When you are aware that you're dreaming, you're not bothered by the things that happen in the dream. Likewise, those people who understand that defilements are also nothing other than a kind of dream are never deceived by those things. Even in a dream, don't see things as separate from yourself, and don't allow yourself to get caught up in the things that happen.

Phenomena appear to exist inherently, independently of our conceptual frameworks, and we deludedly grasp on to them as existing just as they appear. But this simply perpetuates the dreamlike nature of experience of all kinds. When you become lucid in a dream, you begin to recognize that things are not as they appear, and now your challenge is to recognize the extent to which things in the waking state are no more real than a dream.

The most profound and effective way of overcoming sloth and torpor is to make peace with the dullness and stop fighting it! When I was a young monk in the forest monasteries in Thailand and became sleepy during the 3:15 AM sitting, I would struggle like hell to overpower the dullness. I would usually fail. But when I did succeed in overcoming my sleepiness, restlessness would replace it. So I would calm down the restlessness and fall back into sloth and torpor. My meditation was like a pendulum swinging between extremes and never finding the middle. It took many years to understand what was going on.

The Buddha advocated investigation, not fighting. So I examined where my sloth and torpor came from. I had been meditating at 3:15 in the morning, having slept very litte, I was malnourished, an English monk in a hot tropical jungle—what would you expect!

The dullness was the effect of natural causes. I let go and made peace with my sleepiness. I stopped fighting and let my head droop. Who knows, I might even have snored. When I stopped fighting sloth and torpor it did not last all that long. Moreover, when it passed I was left with peace and not with restlessness. I had found the middle of my pendulum swing and I could observe my breath easily from then on.

In the Tibetan Buddhist literature, it is said that one experiences a glimpse of clear light on various occasions, including sneezing, fainting, dying, sexual intercouse, and sleep. Normally, our sense of self, or ego, is quite strong and we tend to relate to the world with that subjectivity. But on these particular occasions, this strong sense of self is slightly relaxed.

Morning Travel

Rising early
to begin the journey;
not a sound
from the chickens next door.

Beneath the lamp,
I part from the innkeeper;
on the road, my skinny horse
moves through the dark.

Slipping on stones
newly frosted,
threading through the woods,
we scare up birds roosting.

After a bell sounds
far in the mountains,
the colors of daybreak
gradually form.

CHIA TAO IN *WHEN I FIND YOU AGAIN IT WILL BE IN MOUNTAINS* | 237

In the Tibetan tradition, dreams are often a way for a person, or an unborn baby, to bridge life in this world with other lives. For instance, in the twenty-sixth week of pregnancy, it is believed that the fetus begins to remember its past lives. At this point, the mother may experience unusual dreams, as if they belonged to somebody else. There may be different settings that seem unfamiliar, yet somehow important. A mother who attends to these dreams may have hints about her child's earlier lives and calling or the child's purpose in this life.

ANNE HUBBELL MAIDEN AND EDIE FARWELL IN *THE TIBETAN ART OF PARENTING*

If there were real benefit in leading a lethargic way of life, we should already have benefited by now because we've had plenty of experience doing that since beginningless time. Enough is enough. Now is the time to set aside sleep and apply ourselves to the Dharma.

CHÖKYI NYIMA RINPOCHE AND DAVID R. SHLIM IN *MEDICINE & COMPASSION*

We have all experienced the fact that a deep emotion—whether positive or negative—can stay with us for the whole day and night, whether we want it to or not. If your first thought of the day is not only noble but is deeply and sincerely felt, it may permeate the atmosphere fo the rest of your day.

There are ways of dealing with bad dreams: the main
technique is to meditate on emptiness, but also, in situations
of fright and discomfort, it is important to take specific
cognizance of the object—the person or being who is
the source of the fright or displeasure—and then cultivate
compassion and love. The best protection is to think,
"Just as I want happiness, so this being wants happiness.
May this being attain happiness, may this being come
to possess happiness!"

Quiet Night

The night is quiet and my room freshly washed.
Beside the folded quilt, I sit tending the fire.
I don't know the lateness of the night.
The flames have burned to cold ash,
but my loving heart hasn't cooled.
Before the cock crowed, we met and talked,
but dreams are vague.

A lucid dream is a perfect laboratory for the first-person study of the mind.

Looking historically at the research on sleep, we see that the main discoveries have all disproved the view that sleep is passive. Neuroscience started off with the traditional idea that sleep is like switching off the lights of the house, and that human beings left alone with nothing to do will fall asleep. Advances in research very quickly made it clear that sleep is an active phenomenon. It is a state of consciousness with its own laws.

FRANCISCO J. VARELA IN *SLEEPING, DREAMING, AND DYING*

At a point in time when I was feeling desolate,
I heard the voice of a cricket very close to my pillow:

At that turning point,
with my head for the last time
pillowed in sagebrush,
I'd have this chirping insect
still be what's closest to me.

The dreams we meet in sleep occupy more than half our conscious life. They are interesting guides and potentially wonderful teachers, which move between realities with ease and can help us open to that mind. They cannot be decoded like riddles (though we may flatter ourselves with trying), yet they can help decode our own riddle, and their substance is the same no-base that utterly holds up and brings forth our life.

SUSAN MURPHY IN *UPSIDE-DOWN ZEN*

Think: "I had a dream like that last night. While various feelings of attachment and hatred occurred, they only arose in that way because my mind was affected by sleep. Of course, when I awoke from sleep those objects toward which attachment and hatred had arisen had not come to this place; not even a trace of them existed. Similarly, because it is affected by beginningless habitual propensities, the mind arises as the various places, bodies, experiences, enemies, and friends in samsara, even though they do not exist. This arising of the various thoughts of attachment and hatred is not even slightly different than it was in the dream. They are equal in appearing to a confused perception, equal in not really existing, and equal in the performance of particular functions and the experience of pleasant and painful sensations, even though they do not exist."

Pure lands and corrupted, unclean lands are both merely coming and going within a dream; how could they be yearned for by awakened ones?

The daytime practice of dream yoga can be approached first from the perspective of classical Buddhist philosophy and then in terms of the relativistic Middle Way. Through the close application of mindfulness, take as your "dreamsigns" anything that appears to be permanent, ultimately satisfying, and as belonging to an independent self. Wake up to the fact that you are conflating your conceptual projections with the immediate contents of experience, and recall the Buddha's statement, "In the seen there is only the seen; in the heard, there is only the heard; in the sensed, there is only the sensed; in the mentally perceived, there is only the mentally perceived."

First, prior to getting up in the morning and before
initiating any tasks, you should armor yourself with the
thought "I shall, in order to make my human existence
purposeful, engage in the practice of the awakening mind
by means of giving and taking (*tonglen*)." When going to
bed, look back and examine whether you have succeeded.
If so, you should rejoice, and with admiration cultivate
joy. If you have not succeeded, acknowledge your
shortcomings and purify your negativity.

If we are attached to something in a dream, it obviously is not going to last, because the dream state is so impermanent. You could say that the pleasure experienced in a dream has even less value, because it is even shorter and less stable than the pleasure experienced in the waking state. Further, the state of dreaming is one of added confusion, because these images in a dream come from the confused images of phenomena we experience in our waking life. It is, therefore, of no use to try to hold on to something that happened in a dream. In the same way, when we practice meditation, various experiences will arise and it is important not to fixate on them or become attached.

Once "Mary" began attending group sittings, and especially during meditation retreats she found herself subject to repeated bouts of intense sleepiness. After a while she consulted a neurologist and underwent sleep studies that determined she had a form of narcolepsy. While her mind was actively thinking she could stay awake, but any period in which her thoughts quieted down seemed inevitably to lead to her falling asleep. The EEG seemed to be telling her she could never enter into those special states of thought-free concentration called samadhi that everything she read said was the goal of Zen. She seriously considered the possibility that she should quit zazen practice entirely, as it was obviously unsuited to the kind of person the neurologist said she was.

One way or another, she kept sitting. She was forced to sit with a true attitude of no gain—all her hopes for practice had been thoroughly undermined by her neurological diagnosis. Yet she kept sitting, somehow still devoted to the practice even though she thought herself forever barred from what others around her would be accomplishing. Then one day, after a weekend retreat, she went to a museum show of calligraphy by old Japanese masters. Suddenly, all her sense of damage dropped away. She was who she was, and in a strange way that was nobody at all. All the old stories by which she had defined herself all those years suddenly seemed empty, just stories she no longer believed in.

After that, nothing changed. She still fell asleep sitting. But also everything had changed. Her problems were just problems, no longer evidence that proved that there was something wrong with her.

It is said that by training in this transitional process of dreaming, since the transitional processes of reality-itself and of becoming are like the dream-state, those transitional processes will be apprehended. Moreover, it is said that if the dream-state is apprehended seven times, the transitional process (following death) will be recognized. These are the instructions on the transitional process of dreaming called "the natural liberation of confusion."

Since the "real world" seems
to be less than truly real,
why need I suppose
the world of dreams is nothing
other than a world of dreams?

In a dream, when you look at a wall, for example, you will see it as being something firm and hard, and if you reach out to touch it, this perception will be confirmed. But the dreamed wall does not consist of any configurations of mass-energy. It has no atomic density, nor does your dreamed body, so there should be no reason why you can't walk right through the wall. Nevertheless, most lucid dreamers have a hard time, at least at their first attempts, walking through walls. Even though they "know" the wall has no objective existence apart from their experience of it, they still can't walk through it. Some have ingeniously found that they can walk through it backward. Another reported that when he first tried this, he made it halfway through the wall, then got stuck, as if it were a gelatinous substance. Many lucid dreamers find it relatively easy to fly, but walking on water and moving through solid objects may be more challenging. In this phase of dream yoga, you keep working at transforming all kinds of dream phenomena, exploring whether there is anything that is objectively resistant to the powers of your imagination. In this way, you begin to fathom the nature of dreaming consciousness and its creative powers.

Dullness in meditation is the result of a tired mind, usually one that has been overworking. Fighting that dullness makes you even more exhausted. Resting allows the energy to return to the mind. To understand this process, I will now introduce the two halves of the mind: *the knower* and *the doer*. The knower is the passive half of the mind that simply receives information. The doer is the active half that responds with evaluating, thinking, and controlling. The knower and the doer share the same source of mental energy. Thus, when you are doing a lot, when you have a busy lifestyle and are struggling to get on, the doer consumes most of your mental energy, leaving only a pittance for the knower. When the knower is starved of mental energy you experience dullness.

AJAHN BRAHM IN *MINDFULNESS, BLISS, AND BEYOND*

It is said in Buddhist scriptures that during the daytime one accumulates propensities through one's behavior and experiences, and these imprints that are stored in the mental continuum can be aroused, or made manifest, in dreams.

One of the most elaborate versions of the conception dream of Maya,
the Buddha's mother, is contained in the Nidana-Katha, *the*
standard Theravada biography of the Buddha:

At that time the Midsummer festival, Asalaha, was
proclaimed in the city of Kapilasvatthu. During the seven
days before the full moon Mahamaya had taken part in
the festivities. On the seventh day she rose early, bathed
in scented water, and distributed alms. Wearing splendid
clothes and eating pure food, she performed the vows of
the holy day. Then she entered her bed chamber, fell
asleep, and saw the following dream.

The four guardians of the world lifted her on her couch
and carried her to the Himalaya mountains and placed
her under a great sala tree. Then their queens bathed her,
dressed her in heavenly garments, anointed her with
perfumes, and put garlands of heavenly flowers on her.
They laid her on a heavenly couch, with its head toward
the east. The Bodhisattva, wandering as a superb white

elephant, approached her from the north. Holding a white lotus flower in his trunk, he circumambulated her three times. Then he gently struck her right side, and entered her womb.

Overnight at a Mountain Monastery

Massed peaks pierce
the sky's cold colors;
here, the trail junctions
with the temple path.

Shooting stars pass
into sparse-branched trees;
the moon travels one way,
clouds the other.

Few people come
to this mountaintop;
cranes do not flock
in the tall pines.

One Buddhist monk,
eighty years old,
has never heard
of the world's affairs.

In Tibet, it is believed that children remember their previous lives until they begin to stand, and that every time the child gets up and falls down, more past incarnations are forgotten and more is learned about this lifetime. When babies smile or cry in their sleep, it is said that is due to their connection to previous lives.

A nightmare can act as a catalyst for apprehending the dream as a dream.

It's much easier to apprehend dreams, too, if you sit up, rather than lie down while sleeping.

We call it "falling asleep," but what actually happens resembles a small death. Waking up in the morning is similar to taking birth into this world for the first time.

According to my own experience, reciting mantras and
doing visualizations do not have much effect during a
nightmare, but as a last resort, remembering compassion and
altruism toward that frightening object brings immediate
peace. The best protection is to protect ourselves from
anger, hatred, and fear by remaining always with the
courage and determination of compassion.

Dreams and Cares

Last night my cares lasted so long
I thought my dreams as long.
So I set off to see you
but awoke before reaching halfway.

At dawn my dreams were so short
I thought my cares as short.
But worry after worry—
I don't know when it will end.

My love, if you also
have dreams and cares,
I would rather that your cares
turn into dreams and dreams into cares.

My body will somewhere fall
by the wayside into a state of
sleep and still more sleep—
like the dew that each night appears,
then falls from roadside grasses.

Strong dreamsigns consist of events that, as far as you know, can happen only in a dream. For example, if you are reading a book and it turns into a squid, that's a strong dreamsign, and if you recognize it as such, you've become lucid. Many other "supernatural events" commonly occur in dreams, but if you fail to apply a critical-reflective attitude to these strong dreamsigns, you will continue to take everything you experience as being objectively real.

Weak dreamsigns are events that are highly improbable but not completely impossible as far as you know. Seeing an elephant sauntering across your front lawn is one example of a weak dreamsign unless you live in the jungles of Sri Lanka or on a game reservation in Kenya. When you experience anything that's a bit out of the ordinary, conduct a *state check*. If there's something in sight that you can read, conduct the state check of seeing if the words change after you look away for a few seconds. If there's nothing of the sort, you can simply take a close look at your surroundings and see whether they are as stable as your normal waking experience. Look out for inexplicable fluctuations that may indicate a dream.

Last night we were reading, bent over a book and absorbing ideas that flashed with surprising beauty. Things were beginning to make sense—in a quiet, intellectual way, at any rate—and that was rare enough amid our usual hurry and agitation. We could see profound matters to pursue, profound matters to test. And then, of course, we got tired, and the evening at last dissolved into fatigue, confusion, and sleep. But something of our delight has not vanished; something has urged us out this far into the fragrant summer air. Let us therefore take up last night's contemplations and find out whether they can stand the daylight.

BHIKKHU NYANASOBHANO IN *AVAILABLE TRUTH*

We have been asleep for countless lives—
now it's time to wake up!

Last night, this mountain monk struck the empty sky with a single blow. My fist didn't hurt, but the empty sky knew pain.

Cloquet hated reality
but realized it was still the only place
to get a good steak.

WOODY ALLEN
(QUOTED IN *HARDCORE ZEN*)

BIBLIOGRAPHY & INDEX BY BOOK CITED

All titles below published by Wisdom Publications.

Numbers in brackets indicate the pages in this volume on which exerpt from this title appears.

The Attention Revolution: Unlocking the Power of the Focused Mind. B. Alan Wallace. 2006. [16, 23, 34, 54, 65, 76, 93, 97, 101, 106, 123, 127, 133, 138, 145, 158, 163, 174, 178, 187, 200–1, 205, 208, 210, 214, 221, 227, 233, 243, 249, 256–7, 270–1]

Available Truth: Excursions into Buddhist Wisdom and the Natural World. Bhikkhu Nyanasobhano. 2007. [5, 29, 58, 81, 131, 180, 203, 224, 272]

Awesome Nightfall. The Life, Times, and Poetry of Saigyo. William R. LaFleur. 2003. [55, 66, 198, 226, 245, 255, 273]

Becoming Vajrasattva: The Tantric Path of Purification. Lama Yeshe. 2004. [230, 269]

The Book of Equanimity: Illuminating Classic Zen Koans. Gerry Shishin Wick. 2005. [79, 128]

Buddhist Psychology (Volume 3 of the Foundation of Buddhist Thought). Geshe Tashi Tsering. 2006. [160]

The Clouds Should Know Me By Now: Buddhist Poet Monks of China. Edited by Red Pine and Mike O'Connor. 1998. [126, 175]

The Connected Discourses of the Buddha: A Translation of the Samyutta Nikaya. Translated by Bhikkhu Bodhi. 2000. [2–3, 14–15, 87, 114–5, 136]

Daughters of Emptiness: Poems of Chinese Buddhist Nuns. Beata Grant. 2003. [26–7, 44, 78, 104, 150, 231]

The Diamond Sutra: Transforming the Way We Perceive the World. Mu Soeng. 2000. [223]

Dogen's Extensive Record: A Translation of the Eihei Koroku. Translated by Taigen Dan Leighton and Shohaku Okumura. Edited and introduced by Taigen Dan Leighton. Introductory essays by Steven Heine and John Daido Loori. 2004. [28, 80, 107, 129, 152, 177, 199, 248, 274]

Dreaming in the Lotus: Buddhist Dream Narrative, Imagery, and Practice. Serinity Young. 1999. [19, 46, 69, 94, 119, 139, 165, 189, 197, 213, 260–1]

Everything Yearned For: Manhae's Poems of Love and Longing. Translated and introduced by Francisca Cho. 2005. [42–3, 74, 92, 117, 146, 173, 195, 220, 242, 268]

The Four Foundations of Mindfulness. Venerable U Silananda. 2003. [103, 125, 148]

Gesture of Awareness: A Radical Approach to Time, Space, and Movement. Charles Genoud. 2006. [109]

Hardcore Zen: Punk Rock, Monster Movies, and the Truth About Reality. Brad Warner. 2003. [275]

The Hazy Moon of Enlightenment: Part of the On Zen Practice Collection. Taizan Maezumi and Bernie Glassman. 2007. [155]

In the Buddha's Words: An Anthology of Discourses from the Pali Canon. Edited by Bhikkhu Bodhi. 2005. [90–1]

Introduction to Tantra: The Transformation of Desire. Lama Yeshe. Edited by Jonathan Landaw. 2001. [51]

Kalachakra Tantra: Rite of Initiation. His Holiness the Dalai Lama. Translated, edited, and introduced by Jeffrey Hopkins. 1999. [172, 194, 219, 241, 267]

Like a Dream, Like a Fantasy: The Zen Teaching and Poetry of Nyogen Senzaki. Nyogen Senzaki. Edited and introduced by Eido Shimano. 2005. [140]

Luminous Mind: The Way of the Buddha. Kalu Rinpoche. 1996. [24–5, 102, 105, 122, 144]

Mahamudra—The Moonlight—Quintessence of Mind and Meditation. Dakpo Tashi Namgyal. Translated by Lobsang P. Lhalungpa. 2005. [11, 41, 63, 86, 112, 135, 159]

Medicine and Compassion: A Tibetan Lama's Guidance for Caregivers. Chökyi Nyima Rinpoche with David R. Shlim, M.D. Translated by Erik Pema Kunsang. 2004. [22, 50, 73, 193, 218, 240, 266]

Meditation on Emptiness. Jeffrey Hopkins. 1996. [171]

Mind Training: The Great Collection. Translated and edited by Thupten Jinpa. Compiled by Shönu Gyalchuk and Konchok Gyaltsen. 2005. [37, 157, 183, 206, 228, 250]

Mindful Therapy: A Guide for Therapists and Helping Professionals. Thomas Bien. 2006. [13, 161, 185]

Mindfulness, Bliss, and Beyond: A Meditator's Handbook. Ajahn Brahm. 2006. [17, 67, 188, 211, 234–5]

Minding What Matters: Psychotherapy and the Buddha Within. Robert Langan. 2006. [9, 60, 83, 110, 132, 156, 182, 204, 225]

Mud and Water: The Collected Teachings of Zen Master Bassui. Translated by Arthur Braverman. 2002. [99, 143]

Natural Liberation: Padmasambhava's Teachings on the Six Bardos. Padmasambhava. Commentary by Gyatrul Rinpoche. Translated by B. Alan Wallace. 1997. [4, 13, 39, 49, 64, 75, 88–9, 116, 137, 147, 166–7, 170, 186, 192, 217, 239, 254, 264]

No River to Cross: Trusting the Enlightenment That's Always Right Here. Daehaeng Sunim. 2007. [209, 232]

Ordinary Mind: Exploring the Common Ground of Zen and Psychoanalysis. Barry Magid. 2005. [42–3, 72, 252–3]

Peacock in the Poison Grove: Two Buddhist Texts on Training the Mind. Geshe Lhundub Sopa with Michael Sweet and Leonard Zwilling. 2001. [21]

Pointing Out the Great Way: The Stages of Meditation in the Mahamudra Tradition. Daniel Brown. 2006. [59, 82]

The Record of Transmitting the Light: Zen Master Keizan's Denkoroku. Translated by Francis Dojun Cook. 2003. [56]

Saying Yes to Life (Even the Hard Parts). Ezra Bayda with Josh Bartok. 2005. [10, 61, 84, 110, 134]

Sleeping, Dreaming, and Dying: An Exploration of Consciousness. His Holiness the Dalai Lama. Translated by Francisco J. Varela. 1997. [1, 12, 18, 30–1, 36, 40, 45, 62, 68, 77, 85, 96, 100, 118, 124, 130, 149, 154, 164, 176, 181, 296, 212, 216, 236, 244, 259, 265}

A Song for the King: Saraha on Mahamudra Meditation. Khenchen Thrangu Rinpoche. Michele Martin, translator of the Song and editor. Commentary translated by Peter O'Hearn. 2006. [38, 184, 207, 229, 251]

Taking the Result as the Path: Core Teachings of the Sakya Lamdre Tradition. Translated by Cyrus Stearns. 2006. [8, 35, 247]

The Three Levels of Spiritual Perception: An Oral Commentary on The Three Visions of Ngorchen Konchog Lhundrub. Deshung Rinpoche. Translated by Jared Rhoton. Edited and introduced by Victoria R.M. Scott. 2003. [48, 71]

The Tibetan Art of Parenting: From Before Conception Through Early Childhood. Anne Hubbell Maiden and Edie Farwell. 1997. [191, 238, 263]

Tibetan Buddhism from the Ground Up: A Practical Approach for Modern Life. B. Alan Wallace. 1993. [98, 121, 142, 151, 169]

Trust in Mind: The Rebellion of Chinese Zen. Mu Soeng. 2004. [162]

Upside-Down Zen: Finding the Marvelous in the Ordinary. Susan Murphy. 2006. [108, 153, 179, 202, 222, 246]

The Way to Buddhahood: Instructions from a Modern Chinese Master. Yin-shun. 1998. [70]

When I Find You Again It Will Be in Mountains: The Selected Poems of Chia Tao. Translated and edited by Mike O'Connor. 2000. [20, 47, 215, 237, 262]

Who Ordered This Truckload of Dung? Inspiring Stories for Welcoming Life's Difficulties. Ajahn Brahm. 2005. [6–7, 32–3, 57, 258]

The Wisdom Anthology of North American Buddhist Poetry. Edited by Andrew Schelling. 2005. [190]

Wisdom Energy: Basic Buddhist Teachings. Lama Yeshe and Lama Zopa Rinpoche. Edited by Jonathan Landaw. 2000. [95, 120, 141, 168]

INDEX BY TOPIC

ABOUT THE AUTHORS

Josh Bartok is the editor of *Daily Wisdom* and *More Daily Wisdom*, and (with Ezra Bayda) co-author of *Saying Yes to Life (Even the Hard Parts)*. He is a Zen priest and a Dharma Teacher with Boundless Way Zen. He lives outside Boston.

Gustavo Szpilman Cutz, a native of Rio de Janeiro, felt qualified to compile this book after many years of intensive sleeping. For two years he served as editorial assistant at Wisdom Publications.

ABOUT WISDOM PUBLICATIONS

Wisdom Publications, a nonprofit publisher, is dedicated to making available authentic works relating to Buddhism for the benefit of all. We publish books by ancient and modern masters in all traditions of Buddhism, translations of important texts, and original scholarship. Additionally, we offer books that explore East-West themes unfolding as traditional Buddhism encounters our modern culture in all its aspects. Our titles are published with the appreciation of Buddhism as a living philosophy, and with the special commitment to preserve and transmit important works from Buddhism's many traditions.

To learn more about Wisdom, or to browse books online, visit our website at www.wisdompubs.org.

You may request a copy of our catalog online or by writing to this address.

Wisdom Publications
199 Elm Street
Somerville, Massachusetts 02144 USA
Telephone: 617-776-7416 • Fax: 617-776-7841
Email: info@wisdompubs.org • www.wisdompubs.org

THE WISDOM TRUST

As a nonprofit publisher, Wisdom is dedicated to the publication of Dharma books for the benefit of all sentient beings and dependent upon the kindness and generosity of sponsors in order to do so. If you would like to make a donation to Wisdom, you may do so through our website or our Somerville office. If you would like to help sponsor the publication of a book, please write or email us at the address above.

Thank you.

Wisdom is a nonprofit, charitable 501(c)(3) organization affiliated with the Foundation for the Preservation of the Mahayana Tradition (FPMT).

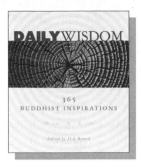

Daily Wisdom
365 Buddhist Inspirations
Edited by Josh Bartok
384 pages, ISBN-13 9780861713004, $16.95

Daily Wisdom draws on the richness of Buddhist writings to inspire you day after day, year after year. Each page, and each new day, reveals another gem of *Daily Wisdom*.

Includes entries by Ayya Khema, Martine Batchelor, Lama Yeshe, Thich Nhat Hanh, Bhante Gunaratana, the Dalai Lama, and more—including the Buddha himself.

More Daily Wisdom
365 Buddhist Inspirations
Edited by Josh Bartok
384 pages, ISBN-13 9780861712960, $16.95

"When you're in need of some bite-sized wisdom or a subject for reflection, this friendly book can help."—*Inquiring Mind*

Entries included are from some of Buddhism's best-known figures: the Dalai Lama, Ajahn Chah, Yangsi Rinpoche, Sylvia Boorstein, Ajahn Brahm, Lama Zopa Rinpoche, and, again, the Buddha himself.

Saying Yes to Life (Even the Hard Parts)
Ezra Bayda with Josh Bartok
Foreword by Thomas Moore
272 pages, ISBN-13 9780861712748, $15.95

"This astonishing collection delivers profound Buddhist wisdom laced with simplicity, practicality, depth, and inspirational vitality."—*Spirituality and Health*

"This is a book of timeless wisdom, one to keep close at hand, not only for the time it takes to read it but throughout life."—Lin Jensen, author of *Bad Dog! A Memoir of Love, Beauty, and Redemption in Dark Places* and *Pavement*

NOW!
The Art of Being Truly Present
Jean Smith
144 pages, ISBN-13 9780861714803, $14.00

"In this timely paperback, the author elucidates the bounties of mindfulness and meditation. On each left-hand page, you will find a brief commentary on a subject that is a natural part of daily living; these are intended to be used pondering, journaling, or for discussion in small groups. On the opposite page are invocations that function as verses for reflection. These reflections and invocations can bring us to a fresh appreciation of being present."—*Spirituality and Health*

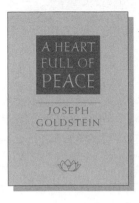

A Heart Full of Peace

Joseph Goldstein
Foreword by the Dalai Lama
128 pages, cloth, ISBN-13
9780861715428, $9.95

This lovely little gift book from bestselling meditation pioneer Joseph Goldstein is proof that big things come in small packages. *A Heart Full of Peace* is a gentle and engaging exploration of the ways that we—any of us—can cultivate and manifest peace as wise and skillful action in the world. Illuminated throughout with lively citations from a host of contemporary and ancient sources including W.S. Merwin, Galway Kinnell, Saint Francis of Assisi, and Thich Nhat Hanh.